The
Ingenious
Angler

Hundreds of
Do-It-Yourself Projects
and Tips to Improve Your Fishing
Boat and Tackle

Keith Walters

International Marine / McGraw-Hill

Camden, Maine • New York • Chicago • San Francisco • Lisbon • London • Madrid
Mexico City • Milan • New Delhi • San Juan • Seoul • Singapore • Sydney • Toronto

International Marine
A Division of The McGraw-Hill Companies

10 9 8 7 6 5 4 3 2 1

Library of Congress Cataloging-in-Publication Data
Walters, Keith, 1930 –
     The ingenious angler : hundreds of do-it-yourself projects and tips to improve your fishing boat
and tackle /
   Keith Walters.
        p.   cm.
     Includes bibliographical references (p.   ) and index.
     ISBN 0-07-137793-X
        1. Fishing—Equipment and supplies. 2. Fishing—Equipment and supplies—Design
     and construction. I. Title.
     SH447.W36 2001
     688.7´91—dc21   2001002880

Questions regarding the content of this book should be addressed to
International Marine
P.O. Box 220
Camden, ME 04843
www.internationalmarine.com

Questions regarding the ordering of this book should be addressed to
The McGraw-Hill Companies
Customer Service Department
P.O. Box 547
Blacklick, OH 43004
Retail customers: 1-800-262-4729
Bookstores: 1-800-722-4726

This book is printed on 70-lb Citation by Quebecor Printing, Fairfield, PA
Design and icon illustration by Carol Gillette
Production by PerfecType and Dan Kirchoff
Photography by Keith Walters except where otherwise noted
Edited by Alex Barnett and Allen Gooch

Trademark information is on page 162.

For my wife of 47 years,
Jean Carole Walters

My ray of sunshine
On the cloudiest day,

My brightest beacon
In the darkest night.

Contents

Foreword

One of the marks of an excellent angler is an inquisitive nature, along with both a desire and a dedication to constantly find better ways to make fishing easier through various tips, projects, ideas, and modifications of tackle, boats, and accessory equipment.

Keith Walters is one of those expert anglers in both freshwater and salt water who are never satisfied with the status quo and who are always searching for ways to make fishing more efficient.

Fortunately for the rest of us, Keith has decided to put the best of the tips, projects, and ideas he has developed, found, tried, and used through the years into this book. In short, it is the culmination of the best tips from years of experience by the experts. I say experts advisedly, since Keith would be the first to admit that all of these ideas are not his, although he is responsible for most of them. The important thing is they are the result of his constantly seeking better ideas for trailering, boating, tackle storage, tackle use, working with accessories, and making simple rigs for all kinds of fishing.

The book is divided into sections that, together with a table of contents, make it easy to quickly find the tip or project you need to solve a problem. Want an idea on mini-outriggers for your boat, fishing tool caddies, tackle storage lockers, marine radio installation, parallel boat docking, launch ramp safety chocks, reel protectors, rod repairs, lure modifications, leader tips, various bait rigs, or pier tackle carts? It's all here.

This is a book that will save you money while making fishing more fun. Just one or two of the hundreds of tips will pay for the cost of this book by saving you money on a fishing project while making fishing easier, safer, and more efficient. Enjoy, learn, and benefit from the information packed in these pages.

C. Boyd Pfeiffer

C. Boyd Pfeiffer has written many magazine articles and fifteen books on fishing.

Acknowledgments

First and foremost, credit for this book must go to my wife, Carole. She organized many years of projects and stacks of illegible field notes. She edited the text and yanked me back on track whenever I went astray. Without a partner like Carole, there would be no *Ingenious Angler*.

Second, there are so many people who helped me along the way by sharing fishing, boat, and tackle hints and tips. C. Boyd Pfeiffer, who wrote the foreword, provided photographs and ideas for some of the projects. It would be impossible to name you all—suffice to say that if your name is in this book, I thank you for your help.

Third, thanks to *Chesapeake Bay Magazine*, *The Fisherman*, *Fishing Tackle Trade News*, *The Mariner*, and *Salt Water Sportsman* for permission to use portions of material I originally wrote for appearance in those publications.

Finally, many thanks to the Fourth Estate—the press—most particularly the other outdoor writers who have helped me every step of the way. I hope that some day, in some way, I can pay it all back.

Introduction

As we mature, our view of what makes a good fishing boat changes. Youngsters, who consider themselves immortal, rate the principal criteria for their ideal fishing craft in this way:

1. Fishability

2. Comfort

3. Safety

At my age, I reverse this order to: safety, comfort, and fishability. This makes more sense, since one must be safe and comfortable to live long enough to enjoy the fishing.

Forty years ago, my first fishing boat was a 12-foot Starcraft aluminum hull powered by a 12 hp Evinrude. I've run OMC motors (Johnson or Evinrude) ever since.

My second fishing craft was a 16-foot Boston Whaler with a 40 hp Montgomery Ward by Evinrude. I had the Whaler ten years and six motors before a dry ride became paramount.

Next, a 20-foot Mako center console with a 140 hp Johnson kept me drier in rough seas. I had the Mako eighteen years and seven motors.

Then I bought a 22-foot Horizon by Angler. Aside from some gelcoat stress cracks, the hull has served me well. It is powered by a 175 hp Johnson Ficht, with a backup motor also on the transom—a 15 hp four-cycle Suzuki, which is also great for flounder trolling!

I recently sold the 14-foot aluminum jon-boat with a 15 hp Johnson described early in this book.

I have included this progression of boats to orient the reader, since many of the ideas and projects in this book may not be in the same order as the above chronologically.

Safety First

Safety is the most important thing to remember as you do any of the projects in this, or any, book. Use common sense.

It is assumed the reader has some skills in working with common hand tools and will exercise utmost care in keeping all body parts away from saws, drills, and other tools that, by themselves, can't tell wood, plastics, or metal from your flesh.

⚠️ **See page 105 for important personal safety tips about working with lead.**

Never, ever, work around the water with electric power tools like drills and saws! My solution to the problem of possible electric shock is to use battery-powered tools where I can and air-powered tools if necessary. It is a pain to drag my air compressor to the dock and use a heavy extension cord to power it, but it would be a lot worse pain to get an electric shock. The air compressor is unplugged and rolled out onto the dock until it needs more air, then I roll it back to its GFCI (ground fault circuit interrupter) breaker for a recharge. On the dock, I have a long air hose to reach the work. (See your electrician for a GFCI breaker installation—it could save you from getting shocked!)

Another way to avoid electric shock is to work on the boat on its trailer in your dry driveway. Larger boats can be modified at the boatyard before putting them in the water. Complicated modifications should be left to the experts.

Small items should be clamped to the workbench or gripped in a vise before drilling or sawing. I see pictures of people drilling sharp pieces of metal like spinner-bait blades while holding the part in their hands, and it gives me the willies. If the drill bit binds, a piece of unclamped metal becomes a rapidly spinning meat slicer—it can puree your hand in a heartbeat!

Look behind or under the work before sawing or drilling. A saber saw cuts a lot deeper than you think. It is possible to cut through a bulkhead, and the pipe or wires behind it, in the blink of an eye.

Working with tools should always be dictated by using common sense. If something can go wrong, it will—often with disastrous results. Be careful!

"Measure twice, cut once" is an old carpenter's saw. Believe it.

Think the project through at least twice and determine if there is anything that could hurt you, then take all the necessary steps to avoid the safety hazards before you proceed with the work. You'll save time, material, and possibly bandages. Take it from me.

Have Fun, but Use Caution

Every project, tip, and hint in this book is the result of problem solving. Tackle to be stored out of the way, lures to be made more effective (we hope!), trailering aids, rod racks—you name it.

The projects are not all-encompassing; they do not solve every problem on every boat or in every tackle box. If they did, this book would be a million pages long and cost thousands of dollars. Included, however, are enough projects to keep the average angler busy for years, as they did me! Each project or idea is explained as clearly as possible, with photographs whenever possible. Projects and tips are numbered; photos are numbered so you can quickly match them up with the appropriate project or tip.

Some may object to the anecdotal style; perfectionists may want nothing but the facts, man, just the facts. But others might enjoy a short break in the data flow to get some background about how the problem arose and how it was solved. Bear with me, since I want this to be a fun book. That's the way I write. An anecdote once in a while can't hurt.

Take your time and select the ideas that appeal or apply to you or your situation. And, most of all, be careful!

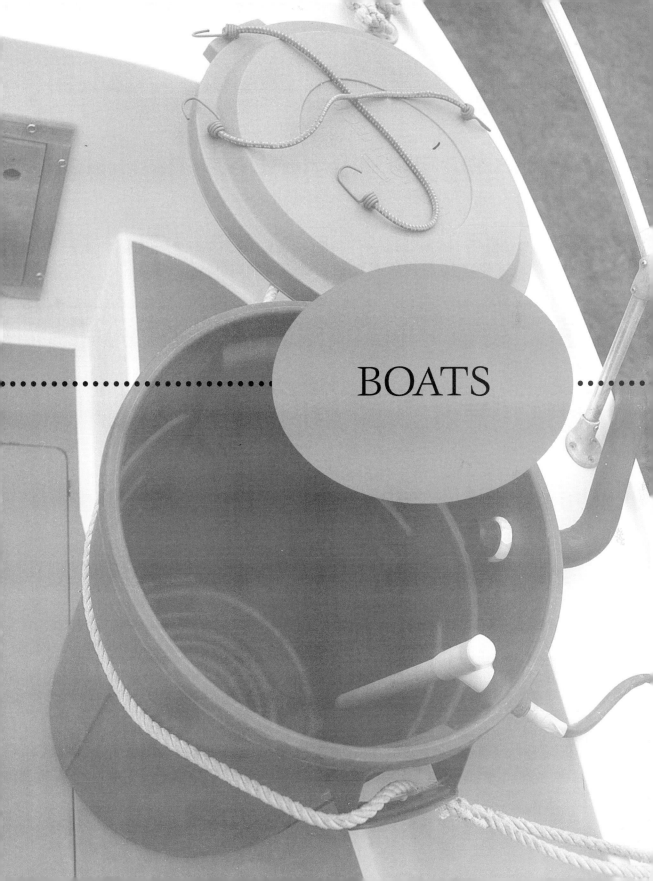

BOATS

A Skinny Water Bass Boat 1

The small aluminum bass boat has many friends. There are as many reasons for owning one as there are anglers.

For some, it's an inexpensive starter boat; for others, it is a way of getting back to basic fishing after experiencing—and owning—big boats. In my case, a neighbor gave me a badly dented 14-foot Montgomery Ward aluminum jonboat. The rivets leaked, and he had replaced them with regular steel

Jack Stovall shows off his "tin boat" pickerel.

nuts and bolts. The oarlocks were worn out. But I'd learned never to look a gift horse in the mouth or a gift boat in the rivets. A few dollars for a few accessories and I knew I would have a neat bass boat.

It leaks a little, my friend warned me. Actually, it leaked a lot. The regular steel nuts and bolts he used to stop rivet leaks do not take kindly to salt water, and that's what we have here in Chesapeake Bay: water salty enough to rust plastic. I replaced the regular steel nuts and bolts with stainless steel ones, caulking around them with marine silicone. I had to use $1/4$-inch-diameter replacement bolts, since my benefactor had already drilled out the old rivet holes, and I couldn't find $1/4$-inch-diameter aluminum rivets.

To check for leaks, I placed the boat upright on sawhorses, half filled it with water, and left it there for a day. Result? No leaks!

Copying a friend's bassin' jonboat, I installed plywood flooring fore and aft to anchor the seats and provide a flat deck to walk on. Stumbling over crosswise ribs is uncomfortable and dangerous.

While casting for bass all day I prefer comfort, so I installed inexpensive folding seats, one for the forward angler and one aft for the captain. None of those slim bicycle seat-leaning posts for me: my back tires too quickly. The flooring and seats are removed for out-of-the-weather storage each winter and put back in the boat in the spring.

I made a cardboard template for the area between the front crosswise seat and the bow and one for the space between the

The author installing swivel seats in the tin boat.

middle and aft crosswise seats. Since the bow of a jonboat sweeps up somewhat, several shallow saw cuts (kerfs) across the underside of the front decking plywood allowed me to bend it to fit the upward curve of the tin.

When the plywood fit the floor, I scribed the position of the raised aluminum crosswise floor braces on the plywood and marked it with a chalkline. I measured the maximum depth I could drill into the raised ribs, then subtracted a little so I wouldn't drill through the boat's bottom and marked the depth on the drill bit with tape. I wanted to drill through plywood and just one thickness of aluminum. The second thickness of aluminum is the bottom. The drill bit was slightly smaller than the diameter of the short Phillips stainless self-tapping tapered-head screws I used to an-

chor the plywood floor. Tapered washers were used to keep the screws from digging too deeply into the plywood.

If I had it to do over again, I would use Quadraplex square-drive stainless steel screws. Repeated use quickly buggers Phillips head screws.

A mushroom anchor fit nicely into the end of a piece of plastic pipe secured near the bow as shown below. The anchor line leads back along the gunwale to a cleat near the rear seat. On the fishing grounds, the anchor dangles from the pipe. While trailering, it is secured in its pipe holder.

Mushroom anchor installation.

Mounting a front electric trolling motor was simple. I fitted an angled block of wood inside the bow so the motor would clamp to a flat surface. I loosened a screw and rotated the tube on the electric motor so both the hand control and propeller faced aft.

I've had second thoughts about a front-mount electric motor. On a bass guide's boat, the captain sits in the front and steers the boat. He gets first shot at the water with his lures. The paying customer gets the second shot at the water. Guide Perry Munro in Nova Scotia mounted his trolling motor on the stern. I got first shot at all those neat little fish hidey-holes. Munro pointed me right at them from his position at the stern. He got second shot at the water—and he caught more fish, on a fly rod yet, but that's another story.

Mounting a new 15 hp Johnson was easy. I simply hung it on, drilled two $\frac{1}{4}$-inch holes through the transom for stainless steel bolts that go through the motor bracket and somewhat permanently secure the motor to the hull. Then I buggered the bolt threads to make it more entertaining for thieves. A motor lock over the clamp screw handles also slowed down potential crooks. Portable items are removed whenever the boat is not in use.

A galvanized trailer pretty much completed my rig, except for some niceties like an old-style flasher depth-finder. I chose a galvanized trailer because I often fish shallow saltwater creeks with the tin boat. The trailer dealer mounted a 2-inch ball coupling on my trailer to be compatible with my big boat trailer. Now, I don't have to change hitch balls to tow different boats.

The tin boat rigged out for bass fishing with electric and outboard motors.

The tin boat has allowed me to fish Maryland's skinny waters, like the Tucka-hoe River, for pickerel, creeks off the upper Choptank for white perch and bass, the Marshyhope (tough pick for bass), and my favorite bass river, the Pocomoke above Snow Hill.

My tin boat gift was not cost free. A new 15 hp Johnson outboard motor, a small electric trolling motor, trailer, plywood, seats, and other accessories were necessities. The full rig cost about $1,500—not a bad price for such a versatile backwater boat, though it would have been cheaper if I had shopped for a used motor and trailer.

Some offshore anglers are returning to their small-boat roots. A friend recently bought an offshore boat so he could chase after tuna and billfish more comfortably. Where does he spend most of his time? In a 16-foot tin boat, banging around stumps and rocks chasing sea trout and striped bass. Go figure.

Pitchfork Propeller Protector   2

Anglers who fish in rocky rivers like the Susquehanna in the upper Chesapeake Bay justifiably worry about their propellers.

Outdoor writer C. Boyd Pfeiffer solved that problem by attaching a pitchfork in front of his outboard motor propeller. You may see a lot of these rigs on small boats on the Susquehanna and many other rocky rivers.

Some welding was required. A piece of bar stock with appropriately spaced holes replaced the round tube that accepted the

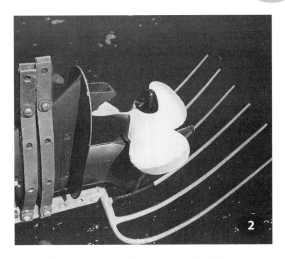

Forks for motors. Hay forks, clamped with strap aluminum to the lower unit of an outboard, will protect props and shear pins from breakage in rocky rivers. C. BOYD PFEIFFER

pitchfork's original wooden handle. Then four pieces of flat steel stock were cut to a length that would wrap around the lower unit (two on either side) of Boyd's outboard motor a few inches above the cavitation plate. Never block your motor's water in-takes! The steel straps were fastened with stainless steel round head bolts, washers, and Nylok nuts.

A few wraps of electrician's tape around the tines closest to the propeller shaft's torpedo-shaped housing protect the housing from excessive abuse.

When the motor is in forward gear, the tilt control is left in the kickup position so it will ride over rocks in the shallows. The steel straps can be painted, but if they finally rust, they are easily replaced. Outboard motors equipped with a pitchfork prop protector might not be as efficient, but their propellers last a lot longer!

Oar Storage on a Tin Boat   3

To keep his oars out of the way and secure while trailering, Jim Walker drilled two holes in the horizontal brace to accommodate his oarlock pins. The blades of the oars are secured with bungee cord.

Handy Tin Boat Rod Rest   4

In small boats fishing rods are always in the way, increasing the likelihood of damage to expensive equipment and also increasing the likelihood that someone will trip over loose gear.

C. Boyd Pfeiffer protects his rod tips with PVC pipe or golf club tubes secured to the bulkhead of his jonboat. A piece of wood shaped to hold the handles is secured to the aft seat, with bungee cord tie-downs keeping the handles in place.

Push Pole   5

Boyd made his own push pole from a 14-foot length of fiberglass rod made for that purpose. One end is pointed. At the opposite end, Boyd added a spring-loaded "duck-

bill" that splays out when the pole is pushed against the water and retracts when it is retrieved for the next push.

Boyd suggests that a 14-, 15-, or 16-foot piece of closet rod is cheaper and would serve the same purpose if properly treated. Duckbills can be purchased from mail order catalogs, and closet rod to fit the duckbill's diameter is available at most lumberyards.

You must make sure your pole is straight and has no snags or splinters that would snag your hands. He suggests two or more coats of varnish after a good sanding. A pole made from wood should be stored inside.

Pfeiffer's rods are kept separated and out of harm's way. C. BOYD PFEIFFER

A 12-foot aluminum telescoping boat hook might appeal to some as a shallow-water push pole, but it could get hung up in rocky bottom and pull you overboard, or come in contact with an underwater electrical cable. For the same expense you could make one of fiberglass.

Push Pole Clamps 6

Push poles are handy to have when you don't want to run a gas or electric motor in shallow water, but a 16-foot pole can be hard to store on a 14-foot boat.

Boyd Pfeiffer's solution was to store the pole on the hull's exterior. He installed two U-shaped clamps, fore and aft, with the open part of the U facing upward. An L-shaped clamp was installed amidships, with a slight turned-down lip at the outside end to hold the pole in place, yet make it easy to remove for use. Boyd covered the center clamp with a piece of plastic hose to prevent abrasion to the pole.

C. BOYD PFEIFFER

More Tin Boat Tips

7 Make a cheap, small-boat anchor by filling a one-gallon container with cement. Put an eyebolt in the concrete before it sets up.

8 Mount a sailboat cam cleat on the bow that will accept your anchor line. Then, mount a regular cleat near the rear seat, handy to the helmsman. Thread your anchor rode through the cam cleat and string it back to the helm through two or three plastic pipe brackets along the gunwales. Hang the anchor off the bow, lower it by giving a tug on the rode to free the cam cleat, and drop the anchor. Secure the anchor rode on the rear cleat. (See photograph on page 78.)

9 When spray painting a skiff for use as a duck boat, first give the craft a background-color base coat. Check with your paint dealer for colors that match the terrain of your area (red clay in Georgia or sandy shorelines). When the base coat dries, cut some leaf-bearing tree limbs and hold them next to the base coat as you spray the contrasting color. The leaf patterns will give a random camouflage look. In the shallows, camo-painted boats don't spook fish as easily as shiny aluminum ones.

10 When making a drag chain on a short rode to slow your drift, make sure the rode is not long enough to reach the motor's propeller! This limits the drag chain for use in shallow water only. With a short rode, it is not necessary to pick up the drag chain every time you move for another drift. See page 76.

11 Tin boat trailers with side or bottom bunks to guide the boat on can be made "slicker" by replacing the carpet with $\frac{1}{4}$-inch thick polyethylene board. Attach it to the wood bunks with countersunk stainless steel screws to keep from scratching the boat hull. Poly helps the boat slide effortlessly, making retrieval easier.

12 Cartoppers need to tie their boats securely to the vehicle. Boyd Pfeiffer drilled one hole in the top of his front bumper and two holes in the top of his rear bumper for eyebolts. His tie-down ropes were terminated with S-hooks, and a spring-loaded levered latch from a boat-trailer store took up the slack. His roof rack was made of 1-by-2-inch laths. I suggested a bracket at the top rear of the car's roof rack that would be a roller—a piece of PVC pipe over a galvanized pipe, perhaps.

13 Make your own jonboat trailer guide-ons as shown at right from PVC pipe. Mine was made from 1-inch ID (inside diameter) PVC pipe, two 90-degree elbows, and two end caps. The U-shaped assembly was attached to the rear cross-brace of the trailer by drilling $\frac{5}{16}$-inch holes through the pipe and the trailer frame for $\frac{1}{4}$-inch stainless steel bolts capped with Nylok nuts with stainless steel washers under the nuts. One could also use stainless steel or plated steel U-bolts if the trailer frame permits. The PVC pipe is about 8 inches higher than the boat gunwale, allowing the vehicle operator to back the trailer down the ramp easier. The PVC assembly is about 4 inches wider than the hull. Some boaters use larger diameter PVC pipe and mount their taillights at the top of the pipe ends for greater visibility. This also keeps the lights out of the water at the launch ramp.

14 Plywood decking is a lot safer and more comfortable in a tin boat than the aluminum reinforcement ribs that are easy to trip over and hard on the feet. Even better, some say, is outdoor carpeting on the plywood.

15 Duck hunters might also cover their aluminum seats with carpet to protect their shotguns.

16 Use an old piece of carpet under the gas tank to cut down on metal-to-metal noise.

17 Boyd Pfeiffer uses an old outboard motor gas tank hose as a manual bilge pump. He removed the motor connectors from both ends of the hose, placed the suction end in the bilge, and put the motor end overboard. The squeeze bulb is placed on the floor near the operator, who simply presses on it with his or her foot to pump the bilge.

Rod Holder Baitboard　　18

An inexpensive, easily stored rod holder baitboard can be quickly made in the home shop. Readily available parts include a 1½-inch OD (outside diameter) chrome-plated brass sink drain tailpipe 12 inches long, a piece of scrap plywood (mine is 9 by 15 inches), and several stainless steel screws shorter than the plywood is thick.

A 12-inch piece of chrome-plated brass sink tailpipe I already had was just the right diameter to fit snugly in my gunwale rod holders. To get a mark as level as possible, I measured when the boat was in the water. I put the pipe into the rod holder, held a level near the top, and drew a "level" line with a permanent black marker. Then I continued that line all the way around the pipe and circumscribed another line about an inch below that.

In the shop, I hacksawed off one end of the pipe at the top "level" line, then cut six tabs, approximately 1 by 1 inch each, down to the lower "level" line with a pair of tin snips.

Next, the tabs were bent and flattened (see photograph top right) so the pipe would support the plywood roughly level when the baitboard was placed in the rod holder. Holes were drilled in each tab. Pencil lines drawn from corner to corner on the bottom of the plywood found the board's center, where the pipe was screwed to the baitboard with screws too short to penetrate the plywood.

After positioning the baitboard in a rod holder, I marked and cut slots in the bottom of the pipe to fit the rod holder's gimbal pins. A slight outboard slant allows bait juices to drip overboard. Two slots hold a fillet knife and an inexpensive pair of stainless steel scissors (see photograph below) I use to cut fragile baits like squid or soft crabs. When the plywood or other scrap board gets too rough looking, simply replace it with another piece of scrap lumber.

A fancier baitboard can be made by sub-

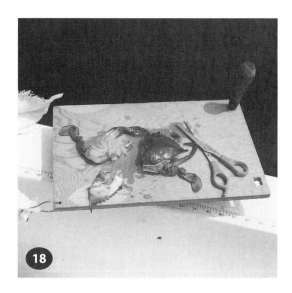

stituting a polyethylene cutting board from a local kitchen store.

Caution:

- Make sure the pipe fits into your rod holder snugly to hold it steady.

- Use short screws that don't protrude to the cutting surface, or you'll dull a lot of knives.

Sink Cutout Baitboard   19

Another handy bait-cutting board for your boat can be easily made from the plastic laminate-covered countertop cutout left over after you install a kitchen sink. A ply-

wood backing will hold up longer in the wet boating environment than will the flakeboard material usually used for kitchen countertops.

Kitchen cabinet installers usually have the cutouts lying around the shop and can sometimes be enticed to give them away or sell them for a nominal fee. Most cutouts will have a pilot hole drilled near one corner to start the saber-saw blade. I turned my sink cutout over and laid out a nice rectangle on the back side with a carpenter's square and a pencil that excluded the drilled hole. An electric handsaw with a plywood blade made a neat cut with the laminate face down. A small pilot hole was

Omar Stoltzfus cleans a king mackerel on the baitboard.

drilled for a saber saw cut to hold the bait knife.

The baitboard can then be laid on an I/O (inboard/outboard) engine box as is, or various devices can be attached to the back of the board to adapt it to your individual boat. To fit my Mako splashwell, I glued two 2 by 4s to the underside of the baitboard far enough apart so they would fit neatly on each side of the splashwell wall.

When the baitboard is not in use, I store it along the side of the boat, held in place by a piece of shock cord. The plastic laminate on my baitboard is easy to clean, doesn't seem to dull the bait knife, and will outlast the backing board.

Mini-Outriggers 20

Shallow-water trolling from a center console boat can be enhanced by adding standard flush-mount gunwale rod holders horizontally in the sides of the boat's console. Normally, these rod holders are mounted vertically in the gunwale tops and hold fish-

ing rods at a slight backward angle. But, rods can be held out horizontally like mini-outriggers when the holders are mounted as in the photographs below and at right.

When trolling in shallow water, one assumes any fish under the boat scoot away to avoid the boat and its propeller. These mini-outriggers place the rod tip and the line well outside the sides of the boat hull. Naturally, the longer the rod, the farther out the rod tips will be. With a bit of luck, trolling lures to the side, and behind the boat a hundred feet or more, places the baits where the fish have stopped to admire the departing boat and will resume feeding. We often caught stripers to 30 pounds while trolling with 10-foot surf rods in the mini-riggers in 10 feet of water down-current from Chesapeake Bay Bridge pilings with 14-inch-long Creek Chub swimming plugs.

In my home river, Maryland's Choptank, locals troll in water so shallow their outboard motor lower units bang over rocks. Placing trolling rods upright in gunwale holders places the baits behind the boat right in the propwash. Getting lures out to the side is more productive.

I once tried regular outriggers in these shallows (and got some funny sideways glances from passing locals), but the slack in the outrigger lines made it almost impossible to hook striking fish. Offshore, where a dropback might be necessary, some slack might be desirable. In shallow water, slack line assures missed strikes. With these mini-outriggers, there is no slack in the line, and a striking fish is easily hooked.

Lures used with mini-outriggers must

run shallow and not dig down like deep swimming plugs. In shallow water, ¼-ounce bucktails decorated with a piece of ripple rind or a swimmertail grub will "float" above the bottom far enough to keep from snagging.

We have also successfully trolled regular surface popping plugs in our mini-outriggers to locate schools of blues and stripers, then we stopped and cast to them with lighter tackle.

Downriggers   21

Downriggers on my 20-foot Mako allowed us to troll lures 30 to 50 feet deep with 14-pound-test spinning tackle. Bluefish caught on downriggers sometimes blew out of the water and jumped across the surface like miniature tarpon.

Great Lakes trollers get even more ex-citement by "stacking" several fishing lines vertically on each downrigger line, but we found one angler per downrigger line was more than enough when good numbers of hungry fish were present.

I mounted two Penn Fathom-Master 600 downriggers, one unit on each side of my Mako's motor well at the transom, pointing straight aft. The downrigger's 2-foot arm kept the cable well behind the outboard's propeller. These units have crank-operated reels with 200 feet of cable, a footage counter, a brake that pays out cable in case the weight hangs up on bottom, and a ball-shaped weight with a built-in line release (see photo on page 16).

Later, I moved the downriggers amidships so we wouldn't have to hang out 2 feet behind the transom to reconnect our lines to downrigger balls (see top photo on page 17). Now they are mounted on the gunwales

Jack Wiley with a "downrigger" bluefish. Downriggers were on the stern.

about 6 feet ahead of the transom with the booms pointed outward. They are much easier to operate in that location. A swivel downrigger mount would be even handier.

With a 10-pound weight on each cable, I rig up leaders and lures. Surgical hose lures and spoons should oscillate or swim to be effective, but they sometimes spin and twist a leader. A ball bearing snap swivel between the release tab on the downrigger ball and the hose lure prevents leader twist. The reel's line is tied to the swivel eye next to the release on the downrigger ball. Fifteen feet of 30-pound-test leader between the hose lure at the business end and the ball bearing swivel completes the rig.

Put spinning or level-wind bass-size out-fits in rod holders, set reel drags loose enough to peel off line, then lower the downrigger weights to where the depth-finder marked fish. Then, retighten the reel drag on light bass or spinning outfits so there is a lot of bend in the rod, and replace rods in the holders. A big bend in the fishing rod will snatch the slack out of the line when the fish hits.

Depth-finders with wide-angle (45-degree) transducers will show downrigger weights on the screen. My narrow 20-degree-angle transducer does not. With no bites after several passes, raise the down-rigger weights in 5-foot increments until you get in the strike zone. Most fish rise up to hit lures several feet above their line of

vision instead of at their eye level.

Anglers who are skilled machinists like Bob Prince can make their own downriggers. Bob machined the reel and arm for the downrigger assembly shown below. He also made a mold for the downrigger weight, and included a stabilizer fin when he poured it. I mounted the base of the unit to a teak step pad on my Mako by removing the pad and recessing four stainless steel $1/4$-20 nuts ($1/4$-inch diameter by 20 threads per inch) in the bottom of the teak block. Next, four $1/4$-20 screws attached the downrigger to the step pad.

Downrigger accessories include remote-control electric motors, rod holders, swivel mounts, "scent-rigger" weights that you can

Downriggers mounted amidships for handier access.

Hard-to-store downriggers can hang from garage ceiling.

pack with chum, flashy prism attractors, speed and temperature readouts, dash panel electronic depth indicators, and a transom mounting bracket that holds up to four downrigger reels, to name but a few. You can stack four or more lines on each vertical downrigger line by adding release clips at intervals.

To try this type of fishing at little cost, simply hang a downrigger ball or sash weight overboard with a line release at the weight; tie it to a piece of clothesline marked every 10 feet with a black Sharpie. Any way you do it, you can double your light-tackle fishing fun with downriggers.

An extra pair of downrigger mount bases and some open space on the garage ceiling combine to make a good place to hang hard-to-store downriggers.

 Make sure the mounting screws for the extra bases go far enough into the ceiling joists that they won't pull out!

Handy Chart Protectors 22

Keeping charts available near the helm and out of the weather is always a problem on fishing boats. For years I kept navigation charts in the zippered clear plastic envelopes sold for that purpose in stationery stores. Chart books fit in the envelopes—even the larger National Oceanic and Atmospheric Administration (NOAA) charts will fit when folded to show the intended fishing area.

To keep charts handy and visible when navigating in bad weather in my first center console boat, I stretched bungee cord across the lower windshield, which blocked part of my view when I sat down to steer the boat. I soon found that a horizontal surface was best for the chart protectors, but they needed to be secured to keep them from blowing away or tumbling to the deck in a bouncing boat. Again, bungee cord was the handiest way to secure the charts.

On my 22-foot walk-around cuddy cabin boat, there is a handy place on top of the hinged cabin hatch that will accommodate two chart envelopes (see photograph below). One of my two envelopes holds a local chart. The other plastic pocket displays both a tide chart and the loran waypoints of my favorite fishing hot spots.

These envelopes are again held in place with bungee cord. I drilled a small hole in the vertical lip on each side of the cabin hatch door to accommodate the bungee cord, tied a simple double overhand knot on the inside, and stretched the cord tight.

The only problem is a transfer of computer or copier print to the inside of the plastic envelope, so everything must be changed at least annually. But, plastic envelopes are inexpensive, and my loran waypoints change almost as frequently as the tides. The advantage of this system is a clear, weatherproof spot handy to the helm.

Tackle Storage Lockers   23

After years of tripping over tackle boxes on boat decks, I finally solved the problem. By combining the empty space inside the raised fiberglass pedestal under the seats of my 22-foot walk-around cuddy boat with plastic storage boxes, I created out-of-the-way tackle storage. An additional benefit is that the plastic boxes can be easily changed with the seasons and available fishing.

There are several ready-made tackle storage systems on the market, but none fit the space I had or my budget. My system is based on inexpensive Plano #3700 Stow-Aways plastic boxes with snap-closing lids, one box for each type of lure (spoon, plug, jig and grub, bucktail, and so on).

The #3700 box would only fit lengthwise into the space I had available. There was room for four plastic lure boxes under each seat, for a total of eight boxes at one time. For different species of fish, I simply exchange the boxes in the boat with others stored in the garage. In addition, I keep four extra lure boxes in a Plano #1296 carrier in the boat's cabin.

To make sure there were no obstructions under the seats, I first cut a 6-inch-diameter inspection hole with a saber saw. If there were any problems at this point, I could have installed a round inspection port and canceled the project. There were no interior obstructions, so I continued. (See photograph below.)

I built two wooden crates, or lockers, of $^5/_{16}$-inch marine plywood, each with three shelves. Each locker accommodates four #3700 boxes. Inside dimensions of the lockers are $9^1/_2$ inches square and $14^3/_8$ inches deep. Spacing is $2^1/_8$ inches between shelves, since #3700 boxes are 2 inches high. Dado cuts $^1/_8$ inch deep in the sides of the lockers accommodate the $12^3/_4$-inch-long shelves. This allows enough overhang to grasp the 14-inch long #3700 boxes. (See photograph at right.)

Boxes got a coating of clear epoxy before being installed.

Shelves are held in place with three-penny finishing nails and epoxy. The lockers are painted with two coats of West System epoxy.

After cutting a $10^1/_4$-inch-square opening (slightly larger than the outside dimension of my lockers) under each seat, I attached 2-by-2-inch hardwood cleats like a "picture frame" around the inside of the openings with epoxy and $1^1/_2$-inch stainless steel #2 square-drive flathead screws. Again, screw holes were predrilled.

Next, the lockers were flush mounted inside the opening and secured with $1^1/_2$-inch flathead stainless steel #2 square-drive screws to the inside cleat. (See photograph at left on page 21.) One of the mounting screws from the seat above was removed

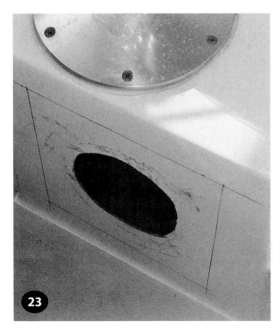

Inspection hole ensured there were no internal obstructions.

and replaced with a longer bolt that mated with a T-nut in the top rear of the locker for additional support. Clear silicone sealer was applied where the lockers met the bulkheads, and stock 12-by-12-inch louvered teak doors purchased from a marine supply store were made ready to mount. (See photograph below right.) First, I milled off the raised lip inside the door frame with a dado blade on my radial arm saw so it would mount flush. The doors were joined to their frames with stainless steel offset cabinet hinges and plastic door catches.

The doors and frame units were attached to the bulkhead outside the lockers with 1-inch #1 square-drive stainless steel flathead trim screws (see photograph below right).

Door frame edges were sealed with clear silicone.

Finally, nylon insect screen was stapled inside the louvered doors to keep out tiny critters.

My smoke-colored Plano #3700 boxes were labeled with a Sharpie waterproof pen on yellow waterproof tape. The newer #3700 boxes are translucent white so you can see your lures better, and the Sharpie pen shows up well on them without using waterproof tape. (See photograph at left on page 22.)

The advantages are flexibility, portabil-

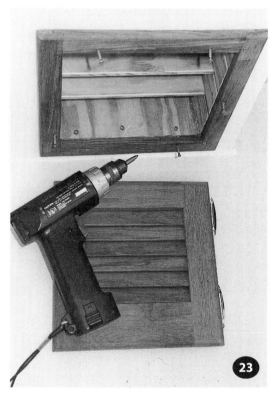

Tackle storage units were attached to the bulk-head.

Individual #3700 tackle boxes can be stored in two lockers or transported in a carrier.

ity, and out-of-the-way storage that lessens the danger of tripping over a tackle box.

I used cleanser to remove layout lines and scuff marks from the fiberglass.

Hidden Lure Storage   24

Captain John Shields of Naples, Florida, has solved the problem of lure storage on his flats boat. These boats are made for shallow-water light-tackle fishing and have limited storage for tackle boxes. Captain Shields covered a vertical bulkhead inside a locker on his boat with indoor-outdoor carpet that allows him to hang his lures by the hooks. He used a type of carpet that does not have a "loop" weave on its upper surface. Looped carpet will capture hook barbs and ruin your day.

He coated the bulkhead and underside of

a premeasured piece of the carpet with contact cement, allowed it to dry, and applied the carpet to the bulkhead. Align the carpet properly before applying pressure, since materials glued with this adhesive are hard to peel apart for realignment purposes.

His lures are out of sight when his boat is unattended—and out of the weather—but they're close at hand when needed.

Capt. John Shields shows his hidden lure storage.

Pipe Structures on Fishing Boats   25

All manner of lightweight structures have been added to boats to raise the angler's point of view, hold various accessories like lights, provide leaning posts, and, in one case of one disabled angler, create a custom-made pipe support to surround and support him so he can cast from the front deck.

Your boat manufacturer or dealer can direct you to a tower fabricator in your area. Some of the largest tower makers have mock-ups and dimensions of most popular boats so they can ship you a custom tower or platform, and your local dealer can install it.

While it is probably best to have a custom welding shop fabricate a pipe tower or rear poling platform, a skilled welder can make his own rig. Tom Seiler of Port Charlotte, Florida, is a skilled welder, so he made his own aluminum pipe "tarpon tower" to give him long-range visibility. He would have made it of stainless steel tubing, but he had previously sold his MIG welder. The Tarpon Hunters Club he belongs to "hunts" tarpon schools with several similarly equipped boats, and when they find a school, they surround it, drop anchor, and fish with dead baits. They are very successful, too, judging by the trip I took with him. (See photograph at right for Seiler's boat.)

Sherman Baynard of Centreville, Maryland, installed a removable push-pole platform for his 17-foot Mako, making his vessel one of the best shallow-water "flats boats" I've seen. He also removed the bow

Brian Seiler scans the Gulf of Mexico for tarpon from the tuna tower while his father, Tom (right), and Bill Perry play a waiting game in the tarpon hunt.

rail and two seats behind the console, giving him plenty of room to fly cast or spin cast lures in Chesapeake shallows. (See top photograph on page 24.)

The upside-down U made of stainless steel pipe used for safety grab handles, which is described in Seatback Safety Handles, project 47, could be fabricated much larger and used for a back brace

Sherman Baynard stands on his push-pole platform.

when fly-fishing all day. Flush sockets for the pipe could be let into the front deck wherever convenient, and the U-brace removed whenever necessary.

Dr. Ed Hahn built a PVC pipe rack to hold his extremely bright night fishing lights 10 feet above the water as required in Delaware Bay. He powers them with a small portable generator. There are so many more uses of PVC pipe on board boats. It can be cut to length and used for rod holders all over the boat, including those attached to bow rails with stainless steel hose clamps, or fastened to bulkheads with screws or nuts and bolts. A slot can be cut in the top to accommodate spinning rod or level-wind reel seats—or cut even deeper to allow for fly reel seats.

Maryland Department of Natural Resources biologist Ben Florence (left) and Dr. Reggie Harrell of the University of Maryland's Horn Point Laboratory bring in a spawning striper.

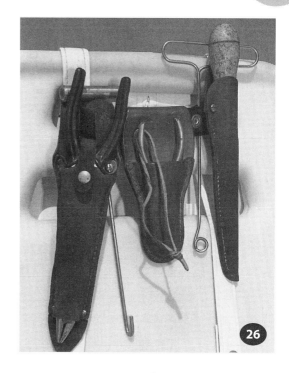

The Maryland DNR's 25-foot "chase boat" is used to pick up huge spawning striped bass cows after they have been electroshocked by another boat. A large tank on board is filled with salt water and tranquilizer so the females can be calmed while in transport to the hatchery where they are spawned out. (See bottom photograph, opposite.)

Many times the chase boats are used at night, hence the lights on a PVC pipe rack that anyone could easily fabricate to his or her own specifications.

⚠ **Do not depend on PVC pipe to support people, since it can break under less stress than the stainless steel or aluminum pipe structures mentioned earlier.**

A Handy Tool Caddy   26

Finding the right pair of pliers or a hook disgorger when fishing is "hot" can be a problem. Murphy's Law says whatever you need most in a hurry will be hardest to find.

To solve this problem, I first looked for the location closest to most of my fishing. On my previous center console boat, it was the back of the seats. On my present walk-around cuddy cabin boat, the seatbacks are again close to the action.

The rest of the job was simple:

- I cut a length of old leather belt that would span the two vertical cushion straps on the seatback and wrapped the belt around both straps to form loops.

- Loops were closed with snaps, but pop rivets (even nuts and bolts) would serve the same purpose.

- Plier and knife sheaths were threaded on the "belt," and I was able to hang "hook-outers" on the belt, too.

- My seatback tool caddy is not only handy to the fishing, but it also keeps knives and pliers in one spot and safely off the deck.

Hard-Sided Tool Caddy   27

Boyd Pfeiffer made this hard-sided tool caddy for his fiberglass boat some years ago. He was concerned that leather sheaths like the previous rig that I made might expose knife blades and "fillet someone," as he explained it.

As shown below, the caddy is made from several layers of plywood with a layer of Plexiglas between tools for visibility. The caddy is bolted together and mounted to a vertical bulkhead.

Boyd simply placed each tool on a piece of plywood and traced around it, then cut the wood around the outline with a saber saw. Thicker tools required two layers of plywood.

The Plexiglas and the plywood layers were cut shorter than the tools so their handles could be easily reached. Stainless steel bolts, washers, and nuts could be used for assembly and through-bolted to a bulkhead. Also short stainless steel screws could be used to assemble the unit, with longer ones in the center to mount it to a bulkhead.

Tools included fishing pliers, a leader crimper, screwdriver, hook file, bait knife, and a fillet knife. The layout could include any tool that would be handy on your boat.

Though Boyd used plywood layers painted white, you could also use polyethylene cutting board for the layers of opaque material. Use a fine-tooth, hollow-ground planer saw blade to get a nice smooth cut. Shape the unit to fit the space available.

Clean your tools before replacing them in the caddy, or fish slime could give the unit an unpleasant odor in a short time.

Convenient Lure Keepers   28

Most of us have several favorite lures we use on a continuing basis. Rooting around in a tackle box when we want to change a lure is out of the question, and it takes too long when the fish are biting.

For years, I used a piece of bungee cord stretched crossways behind my center console windshield. The large saltwater poppers we used then were hung by their tail hooks. In recent years, we use smaller lures, bucktails, knife-handle spoons, and single-hook plugs that have been converted from baits that came with two trebles.

Sherman Baynard wrapped a piece of foam pipe insulation around the grab rail on his center console and secured it with stainless steel hose clamps. Nylon cable ties

C. BOYD PFEIFFER

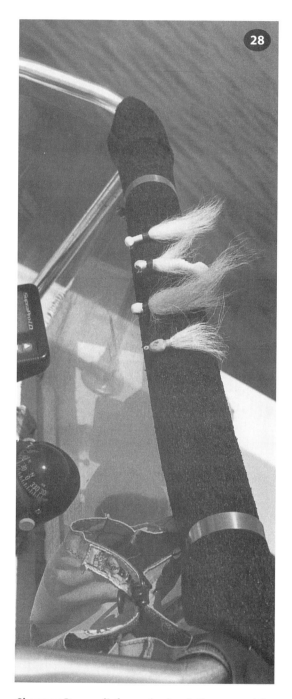

could also be used. Sherman's favorite small bucktail jigs are always handy right in front of the steering station, as shown at left. Bass anglers also use pipe insulation attached to the pedestal of a bass boat seat to keep lures in use handy. The same insulation is used around the outside rail of a pipe T-top as a fly rod cushion for rods stored vertically alongside the center console and could save a delicate rod for a wild caster.

Lures with treble hooks go inside the hinged fly box, and single-hook baits like bucktail jigs are simply stuck in the sides of the box. A piece of fairly dense plastic foam from a packing box could also be used, but some of the loose-grained plastics tend to fall apart easily.

To keep the fly box from flopping around or blowing away, I keep it under the piece of bungee cord that secures my chart and tide table plastic envelopes (see Handy Chart Protectors, project 22).

Sherman Baynard's foam pipe insulation around the grab rail of his center console boat to hold his lures.

A foam plastic fly box I won at a fishing fund-raiser works great as a handy temporary lure keeper.

Other Lure-Keeping and Storage Ideas

29 A clear partitioned plastic box with a lid can be placed near the angler for the "hot" lures of the moment. Pieces of rubber conveyor belt glued to the bottom of the box keep it from skidding.

30 Small compartments in the top of Plano Guide Series tackle boxes have a clear partitioned box built into the top of the larger tackle box.

31 Bass anglers often clamp a piece of pipe insulating foam around the pedestal of their seats or leaning posts to hold favored lures.

32 Clay Gooch of Saint Michaels, Maryland, clamped pipe insulation around the center pipe braces under his T-top to hold lures.

33 A small compartmental plastic box can be rigged as a "belly box" with a belt for wade fishing. Commercial models are available in fly-fishing catalogs.

34 Steel shelves in the garage are winter storage for Plano #3700 boxes and other plastic boxes of boat gear.

35 Heavy-duty zipper-lock plastic bags in a variety of sizes keep lure hooks from snagging.

36 Department stores sell a variety of plastic containers in all sizes to fit your storage needs:

- Laundry baskets store anchors rigged with chain and rope.

- Small watertight boxes can be used for first-aid materials.

- Use plastic shoe boxes to store large offshore lures.

- Larger storage containers hold rolled or folded plastic side curtains or life preservers.

- Golf club tubes or PVC pipe store rolled charts.

Ready-Rigged Fly Rods on a Boat 37

Most under-gunwale rod holders won't accommodate ready-rigged 9- or 10-foot-long fly rods. While storing a separated two-piece fly rod is easy, it can be difficult to rig when fish are breaking all around the boat.

On my 22-foot walk-around cuddy, I use hook and loop wraps to secure a 9-foot fly rod to the inboard side of the bow rail stanchions. These wraps can be purchased in boat stores or made at home with scraps of boat canvas and pieces of hook and loop fastener.

My wife made several wraparound strip fasteners, about 10 inches long and 1½ inches wide, of doubled and sewn Sunbrella boat canvas. She then sewed a 2-inch patch of "hook" on the inside at one end and a

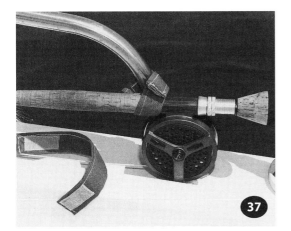

37

2-inch patch of "loop" on the other end on the outside. Length and width can be adjusted as needed.

In use, I tuck the fly rod inside the bow rail, then wrap one fastener around an upright and the fly rod near the reel seat and another near the rod tip and an upright support near the bow. This system has held my fly rod securely in some really rough water. When I spot breaking fish, I simply pull off the fasteners and my rigged fly rod is ready for action!

Tips for Fly-Fishing Aboard Boats

38 "Use a large plastic laundry basket on a boat's deck as a stripping basket," says Boyd Pfeiffer. "Put about an inch of water in the bottom of the basket to stabilize the fly line; the extra weight will also keep the basket from sliding around."

39 Cleats on boats attract fly lines. Capt. Norm Bartlett of Baltimore tapes a rubber snubber, minus the hooks, to a cleat and lets it dangle over the cleat ends.

40 Fly fishers often snag their fly lines and leaders on various boat projections like cleats, cooler handles, or rod holders. Lefty Kreh carries a roll of masking tape with him to cover these snags temporarily. Lefty also occasionally uses a piece of netting as a cover. Boyd Pfeiffer made removable covers out of pieces of packing foam hollowed out to fit over cleats and other parts of the boat. D. L. God-

dard uses a large, wet beach towel over snags for the same reason.

41 Cover the outside rails of a boat's T-top with foam pipe insulation to protect fly rod tips.

42 Fly shop owner Joe Bruce of Baltimore made the stripping basket below from a medium-sized laundry basket, attached low to his side (like a gunslinger's holster) by bungee cord ties.

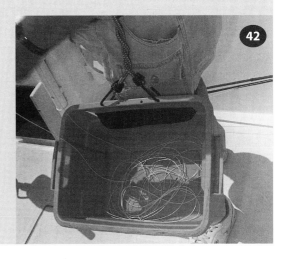

42

43 I made a stripping basket from an old plastic dishpan by cutting slots in its side. A 1-inch-wide nylon web belt was threaded through the slots to go around my waist.

44 A piece of outdoor carpet laid on the boat's deck will keep stripped fly line from tangling. Be sure to keep feet off the line!

Versatile Live Baitwell   45

Most anglers have an occasional need to keep baitfish alive, but all of us don't have the space to make a permanent livewell installation in our boats. My solution to the problem is an easily removable, inexpensive live baitwell system that takes little space in the boat and stores ashore when not needed.

Most seawater circulating systems have three basic parts:

1. A livewell. I use two: a 32-gallon plastic trash can and lid serves for large baits like live bluefish for king mackerel, and a smaller 20-gallon screw-top plastic jug is ideal for minnows and silversides.

2. A pump to move the water: mine is a small 400 gallon per hour bilge pump attached to the lower leg of my outboard motor above the cavitation plate.

3. Piping to connect the pump to the livewell and provide a drain overboard: input lines are made of ¾-inch PVC pipe and fittings attached to an old ¾-inch gar-

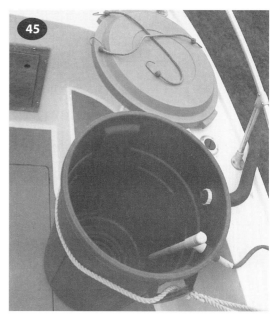

32-gallon livewell.

den hose with couplings. The overboard drain is an old automobile radiator hose.

Livewell: First, I determined the locations for the holes in each livewell by placing it in a suitable location in the boat. I drilled

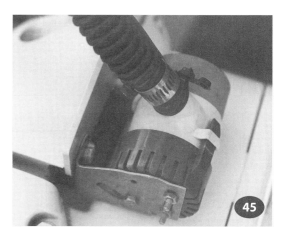

Small bilge pump mounted on lower leg of outboard motor.

two holes with a hole saw in the side of the trash can (and the jug, too) about 4 inches below the lip. A 1³/₄-inch hole fits the 1¹/₄-inch ABS pipe-to-male-thread adapter that inserts into the auto radiator hose overboard drain, and one 1¹/₄-inch hole fits the ³/₄-inch PVC input water pipe.

A short piece of ³/₄-inch PVC input water pipe extends through the smaller hole in the side of the livewell. This connection was left uncemented so I could remove it later. Outside the hole, a PVC pipe-to-male-thread fitting connects to a female garden hose repair coupling. A suitable length of ³/₄-inch hose connects to the bilge pump. Once the garden hose couplings are installed, a short length of garden hose can be used to extend the distance between the bilge pump and the livewell.

Inside the livewell, a 90-degree, ³/₄-inch PVC ell and an 18-inch pipe extension angles downward to provide fresh seawater to the bottom of the livewell. Then, the water flows upward to drain overboard from the top. This removes fish gurry and scales. Very little water sloshes out if the can's lid is secured with a piece of shock cord. An aquarium-sized dip net or a trout net will reach the baitfish easily.

Pump: An L-shaped stainless steel plate has appropriate holes drilled to attach the small bilge pump to the lower leg of the outboard motor above the cavitation plate. Electric 12-volt wiring was extended by soldering longer wires to the bilge pump wiring, and heat-shrink tubing covers the connection. A polarized male plug was attached to the longer wires, and a mating female receptacle was installed on the bulkhead above the boat's battery compartment. Be sure to maintain correct wiring polarity—on my pump the brown wire with an in-line fuse holder goes to the positive battery terminal and the white wire is connected to the negative side. On other pumps, the black wire is negative. Be sure to read the directions or wiring diagram.

Exterior Piping: One obvious problem is the pump is out of the water when the boat is on plane. To solve that problem, some anglers attach a piece of ¹/₂-inch copper pipe to the transom so that the open end of a 90-degree ell will face into the slipstream rushing from under the boat. A Y-valve supplies water from the copper pipe when the boat is on plane or from the pump when slow-trolling or at anchor.

Another option is to substitute a T for the manually operated Y-valve and include a one-way valve to prevent water from draining back overboard through the underway pickup when the boat is at rest.

The 20-gallon jug I use on the newer 22-foot boat (see left photograph on page 32) is basically the same as far as plumbing and wiring are concerned. I clamped a piece of ¹/₄-inch galvanized hardware cloth over the drain to keep minnows from escaping. I also drilled a ¹/₁₆-inch hole near the top of the PVC water supply pipe just inside the jug so the water wouldn't siphon back overboard.

Running a small bilge pump all day on the engine-starting battery can run it down. A separate battery for the pump or a dual battery hookup provides an extra measure of safety.

20-gallon livewell.

My live baitwell system is easily removed and stored when it is not needed. All the parts store in an onion sack, and the trash can is used as such. The 32-gallon can will keep bluefish baits active and vigorous all day, and the smaller 20-gallon jug keeps even very fragile baits like silversides alive and frisky.

Gaff Keeper 46

Shock cord is used for many things on our boats, but I found that one of the best uses for it is to keep a 6-foot gaff handy and safely stored.

After placing a gaff in several locations in my 20-foot center console Mako, I decided that one of the handiest places was just above the under-gunwale rod storage. Next I considered several ways of keeping it in place when the boat is underway in rough water. Stainless steel spring clips or brackets would protrude too far into the narrow aisle alongside the console and their sharp metal edges could threaten trousers or legs.

My solution was to drill two holes through the boat's inner sidewalls for the shock cord that would support each end of the gaff, or a total of four holes, slightly larger than the diameter of the shock cord. Before drilling, I made sure that I could get to the back of the sidewalls to tie knots in

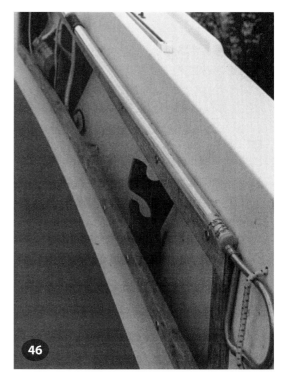

the shock cord. A suitable length of shock cord was knotted on one end and the unknotted end was passed through one of the holes from the back side, then threaded through the other hole. After pulling that end tight from the back to provide suitable tension, I tied a knot in it. This was done for each end of the gaff.

The gaff is stored under the loops in the shock cord, safely out of the way.

⚠️ **A stainless steel spring wire coil, attached to the gaff hook, covers the needle-sharp hook point until the gaff is needed.**

Seatback Safety Handles   47

Adding grab handles to the backs of the seats on my center console Mako solved a potential safety problem. There is nothing for a passenger standing in the back of my boat to grab if the person driving hits the throttle suddenly. I found this out the hard way; by the next weekend I had safety handles installed.

My safety grab handles were made of stainless steel ¾-inch ID stainless steel pipe, bent into a U shape for me by a friend with a conduit bender. To fit my boat seats, each handle is 11 inches wide and 14 inches high, outside dimensions. Your dimensions may be different.

The U-shaped handles were mounted on the backs of the seats with the open side of the U facing downward. I allowed 2 inches of clearance between the top of the seat and the top of the handle. To allow 1 inch of

clearance from the seatback, I made four standoffs 1 inch long for each seat handle from the same stainless steel pipe, for a total of eight standoffs. One end of each standoff was scalloped so that it would fit against the curved pipe of the handle.

Holes to accommodate the ¼-20 by 3-inch-long stainless steel cap screws were drilled 1 inch and 6 inches from the bottom of the inverted U handle. After positioning the handles properly on the seatback, I drilled bolt holes through the seat. Cap screws were inserted from the seat side, and the seatback cushion covered the screw heads for comfort. Then, I cut the cap screws to length and used rounded cap nuts on the handle side for a nicer appearance. For additional safety, I put a dab of epoxy in each cap nut before assembly.

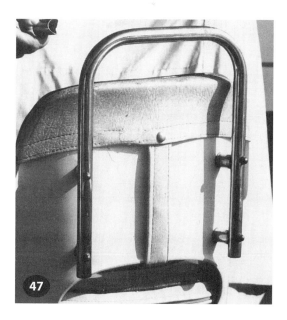

Mounted to the back of a standard boat seat, a U-shaped handle provides a handy safety bar.

Rod Holders 48

Rod holders on boats keep the long wands out of the way yet handy to the angler. Those who grab up a bundle of rods and dump them in a tangled pile on the boat will live to regret it, most notably when fish are breaking water all around the boat, and rods, lines, and lures are permanently entwined.

Most midsized fishing boats today have rod pockets under the gunwales. My 22-foot walk-around cuddy cabin hull has no under-gunwale rod pockets. The longer I have the hull, the more I like the plain bulkheads in the fishing area. Like most anglers in a hurry, I once simply tossed a bundle of rods in the starboard side walkway around the cabin. It seemed like a logical place—the VHF-FM radio antenna is on that side and no one walks around that side, anyway. So, I installed a six-rod holder on that side where there had always been a tangle of rods. (See project 49 for detailed instructions on building a six-rod holder.)

Next, in the cabin, I installed two sets of teak four-rod holders on the bulkheads beside the bunks with short stainless steel square-drive screws, plus epoxy. Mounting gunwale rod holders was quite a challenge, but I think just about anyone handy with tools can do the job. I first determined the best locations for gunwale-top rod holders. Then, I lightly penciled four positions for the holders, two on each side on the gunwale tops. I checked my measurements from the transom so the holes were evenly placed. The aft two holders faced the stern,

and the front ones were angled outboard slightly so their rod's lures would track outside the rear rods.

Luckily, the new rod holders came in an angled plastic package that also served as an excellent drill guide, as shown in the top photograph, opposite. A $\frac{1}{4}$-inch hole was drilled in the center of the bottom of the holder package, and an 18-inch-long, $\frac{1}{4}$-inch-diameter drill bit was aligned through the center of the clear plastic package, which when placed against the gunwale top luckily gave the same, correct angle for the rod holders. Pilot holes were drilled in the gunwale top for a hole saw's guide bit.

⚠️ **Do not use a hole saw without this centering bit—it can whip around out of the hole and hurt you!**

With the hole saw's guide bit aligned in the pilot hole, a $1\frac{3}{4}$-inch hole was drilled in the gunwale top for each rod holder, as shown in the bottom photograph, opposite. I used an electric drill for this job, since the hole saw required so much power.

⚠️ **The boat was on the trailer—never use a 110-volt power tool aboard with the boat in the water! In that case, use only battery-powered or air-powered tools.**

My hull was packed with foam flotation all the way up under the gunwale, so it required a lot of digging to get enough space for the rod holders. Next, I fit the rod holders in place and drilled pilot holes for three mounting screws for each holder. To keep water from running into the foam inside the gunwale, I taped the bottom end of each

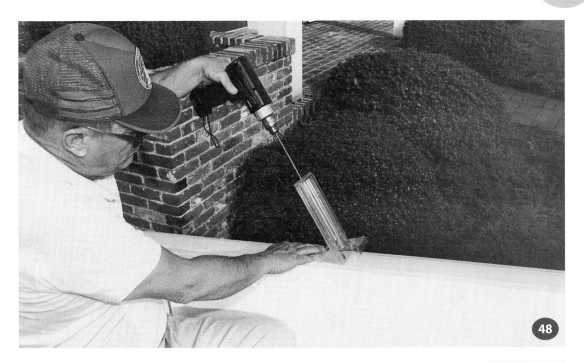

Top: *The author drills the pilot holes for the flush-mounted gunwale rod holders.* Bottom: *The author drills the holes in the gunwale top for a rod holder.*

rod holder, set it up vertically, and carefully poured in a thin coat of epoxy to seal the bottom, as shown below.

When the epoxy set up, the rod holders were screwed down in place, and their rubber covering flaps secured over the rod sockets.

Next, the flat plates for two stainless steel demountable holders were secured, one on each side, to the cabin's exterior bulkheads. The holders are stored in the cabin unless needed for two rods sticking out to the sides when trolling.

Two more bulkhead-mount tube holders were screwed to the aft bulkhead, and a recessed rod holder was mounted on the after-surface of each side of the cabin bulkhead, both facing aft. These are handy when the seats are rotated to face the stern for drift-fishing. The hull came with only two rod holders—surface-mounted tubes installed on an aft bulkhead. Now, I can store

Securing the rod holders in place.

twenty-six rods in holders, although I only use about eighteen different rods on a given fishing day!

All of those already installed on the boat were commercial rod holders, but someone handy with PVC pipe or teak can make rod holders for about any placement ashore or aboard. For instance, I made PVC rod holders for a fishing bench at the end of my dock, and I've seen teak rod holders mounted in beach-buggy ceilings that rival the nicest factory-mades.

Jim Price has rod holders of PVC pipe recessed into the front deck of his 20-foot Mako center console fishing boat (see top photograph, opposite). They keep rods out of the way of his bimini top, which is always up.

Other anglers make PVC rod holders for their boats, and mount them in places that are out of the way, yet accessible. Some beach anglers have adapted PVC pipe for rod hangers on the "bow" of their favorite sand vehicle, but surf angler "Peanut" Sullivan of Berlin, Maryland, mounted rod holders angling aft on each side of the rear fenders on his Chevy Blazer beach buggy.

Surf anglers often use 3- or 4-foot pieces of $1\frac{1}{2}$-inch-diameter PVC pipe for sand spikes. They cut one end on a 30- or 45-degree angle so it will penetrate beach sand, and cut a slot for a reel foot in the opposite end. Shorter versions are used as rod holders on the front of beach buggies so ready-rigged outfits are handy to the action. Sand the burr off the inside top rim of the pipe until it's smooth so it doesn't abrade your rod handles.

Jim Price's bow-mounted rod holders.

Home-brew PVC pipe rod holders should have two mounting holes to stabilize the holder and keep it from turning sideways under stress. Drill a small hole in one side of the pipe to accommodate the screw size you will use, then drill a larger hole opposite that one large enough to accommodate a screwdriver. Repeat those holes far enough apart to assure stability when mounted. For mounting, I use tapered-head, square-drive stainless steel screws recessed flush so rod handles aren't damaged when bounced around in a seaway. A lengthways slot can be cut for an inch or

Capt. Mike Murphy displays a nice trout caught on a rod stored in one of the many rod holders installed on his boat.

two from the top of the holder to engage a spinning or level-wind reel foot and keep it from spinning around in the holder.

I have also used 1⅝-inch ID thin wall plastic pipe made for home central vacuum systems for rod holders. It is easy to work with, but it won't take as much abuse as schedule 40 PVC water pipe. Thin wall tube can be flared at one end by heating it in boiling water or, if careful, with a heat gun and rotating it around a heavyweight tin funnel. This tubing can also be used for light duty sand spikes or rod holders in a jonboat.

Build a Six-Rod Holder   49

As explained in the previous project, the ideal place to toss a bundle of rods when loading my walk-around cuddy cabin boat seemed to be the starboard walkway alongside the cabin. Rods, lures, and lines were often tangled together when we arrived at the fishing grounds. It seemed to me that a rod holder could be built for that same area, since no one could walk around the cabin on that congested side anyway.

A little work with a drill press and a radial arm saw, plus some PVC pipe, a piece of high density polyethylene, and some stainless steel screws went together easily; I made an inexpensive six-rod holder.

First, a 24-inch-long piece of high-density polyethylene ¾ inch thick by 2½ inches wide was shaped into two crosspieces that would hold the individual rod holders (see photograph above for parts layout). A centerline was drawn lengthways from end to end, and six marks were made along that

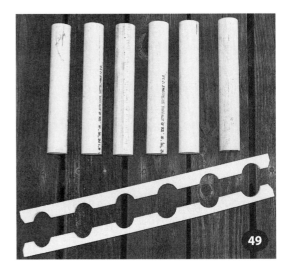

Parts for six-rod holder.

centerline for six 1⅞-inch-diameter holes, about 4 inches apart on centers. After those holes were drilled with a hole saw, the piece was sawed in half lengthways to make the two scalloped pieces that would hold the PVC pipe holders. Sharp corners that would be exposed were rounded off.

Next, six pieces of 1½-inch-diameter schedule 40 PVC water pipe were cut to a length of 12 inches on a radial arm saw with a hollow-cut planer blade.

Then, a tapered slot was made at one end of each rod holder to accommodate the reel seat when a rod is stored in the holder. Another slot with straight sides is then made on the back side of the pipe opposite the tapered one to accept the "finger" on a trigger stick rod. A ¾-inch-diameter hole saw was mounted in a drill press, and a hole centered on the pipe was made 3 inches from the top of the pipe. (See top left photograph on page 39.)

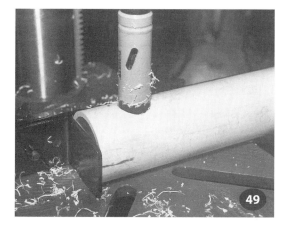

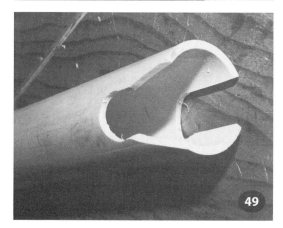

Top: *Drilling the bottom of a reel foot slot with a hole saw.* Middle: *Cutting a tapered slot for reel foot.* Bottom: *Rough-cut slots as mentioned in text.*

 Make sure a fence to the drill press's platform secures the PVC pipe so the hole saw doesn't bind in the hole and spin the work piece around. The drill press has enough torque to cause an injury. Another hole is then drilled opposite the first.

The PVC pipe is then secured on a radial arm saw so two slots can be cut, one tapered, the other with straight sides, as mentioned earlier. The sharp edges of the slots should be sanded so they won't mar fishing equipment. (See photographs at left.)

The "front" side of each piece of PVC pipe is then marked so $1/2$-inch holes can be drilled 6 inches apart for access to the smaller mounting screw holes in the "back side." When assembled, this will place the two scalloped mounting strips about 6 inches apart, with the PVC pipe rod holders secured to the strips through the "back" holes with stainless steel tapered-head square-drive screws. The larger front holes allow easy access for drive bits with an extension. (See photograph below for assembled unit.)

Completed six-rod holder.

To mount the unit on a bulkhead, remove the shorter temporary screws from the four holes at each corner of the unit and replace them with screws long enough to penetrate the mounting surface.

Honeycomb Plug Holder   50

There is no joy in having a lively fish attached to the tail hook of your two-treble hook plug when the other hook is embedded in your finger. To avoid this painful embarrassment, I devised a system that keeps me at a safe distance from treble hooks and sharp-toothed fish.

My system begins with a spinning or bait-casting outfit and some treble hook plugs. I rearm my plugs with sharp stainless steel treble hooks—or a single tail hook for catch-and-release fishing. For toothy fish, I tie about 24 inches of braided wire leader directly to the lure with a figure-eight knot or crimp a loop with leader sleeves. At the end of the wire leader I make another loop that snaps to the end of my fishing line.

For toothless fish that are to go into a cooler, a heavy mono leader could be used. If we have found and hooked up with big, toothy bluefish, we leader the fish into the cooler and slam the lid with the wire leader sticking out. Then, we can safely unsnap the snap swivel at the end of the running line and snap on another plug and get back in business. Lures are retrieved when the fish calms down. To keep the plugs from tangling in this melee, I made a honeycomb plug holder from $1^5/_8$-inch ID PVC electrical conduit with $^1/_2$-inch sheet PVC for the bottom and back. My holder has been mounted on two boats, in back of the seat on my 16-foot Whaler and inside the anchor locker door on my 20-foot Mako.

50

Plug holder mounted on the back of the Boston Whaler seat.

Plug holder mounted on the back of the Mako anchor locker door.

To make the plug holder, I cut 21 pieces of the PVC conduit into 8-inch lengths and arranged the pieces in staggered rows, like a honeycomb, for strength. The bottom and the mounting straps in the back were cut from the sheet PVC. All parts were assembled and glued with standard PVC cement. Small holes were drilled in the bottom of the tubes for drainage.

When I transferred the holder from the Whaler to the Mako, I simply cut off two of the end conduits so the holder would fit the anchor locker door.

A plug holder like mine could be assembled from many other materials: schedule 40 PVC water pipe, Plexiglas, copper, or even stainless steel.

Console Top Organizer 51

A compartmental Plexiglas tray about 2 inches deep, 6 inches wide, and 13 inches long helps organize all the miscellaneous "small stuff" that used to rattle around on (and eventually fall off) the top of the center console on my fishing boat. A few small squares of double-sided foam tape of the type artists use to mount pictures can hold the tray down in rough seas but are easy to remove.

The many small sections in the tray accommodate the variety of tiny items one usually has to dig for in a tackle box or pockets. The tray was originally labeled as a cosmetics organizer, but a similar tray could be built for your boat. Almost any material the tackle tinkerer has at hand would do the job. Even a kitchen drawer insert for organizing knives and forks will work. The only change I made was to drill a small hole in the bottom of each section for drainage.

If you need some special design for a hard-to-fit place, you can make your own organizer from ¼-inch-thick Plexiglas sheet. Check with a plastics shop for the proper sawing technique and the proper solvent for your material.

A recent inventory of the contents of my organizer revealed the following items: six sizes of snaps and snap swivels, four different types of sinkers in assorted weights, several small spoons and bucktail jigs, two sharpening stones, a stainless steel multi-function knife, an extra boat drain plug, and a boat gas cap key. If a small item needs to be handy, it's in my organizer!

Several Electric-Motor Installations   52

Anglers drifting for flounder and other bottom-feeders know their bait must be moving across the bottom, and they must cover a lot of bottom unless the fish are really thick. But when wind and tide are slack, a minnow is allowed to sit still on the bottom too long—it gets a chance to look around and find something to hide under. Keep the bait moving, say the experts.

A small outboard motor will work, or you can use a small, quiet electric motor and avoid the noise and oil fumes from a two-cycle gas engine. Several years ago, I bought a transom-mount Minn Kota 35M electric for the 14-foot jonboat I use for bass fishing in protected waters. Later, I found the same motor also moves my 22-foot fiberglass hull on Chesapeake Bay at flounder-catching speed on days when we are becalmed by wind and current.

Small electric motors usually have alligator clips on the power leads, and some anglers carry a spare deep-cycle battery to use with their small motor. I substituted a polarized heavy-duty plug for the clips, then mounted a compatible receptacle just above the two-battery compartment near the transom on my 22-foot boat. I caution you to use wire heavy enough to handle your electric motor's considerable current draw for the leads between the battery and receptacle, and use a proper fuse. Undersize wire can cause a fire when overheated. Byrd Industries calculated that the thrust on a 12-volt motor, with about 18 feet of battery cable, will increase about 34 percent when the heavier 4-gauge wire is substituted for 12-gauge. Byrd also suggests keeping the battery cable as short as possible.

By using 4-gauge wire instead of 12-gauge, you could improve performance beyond 40 percent. Also, determine whether your electric motor needs 12, 24, or 36 volts, then follow the motor's installation di-

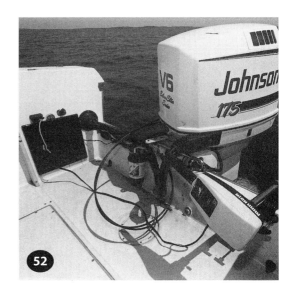

52

rections and wiring diagrams accordingly. To use the small electric motor on my small jonboat, I have a spare battery with a compatible polarized receptacle mounted on the top of its plastic case.

Technically inclined anglers will notice that in the stern of my 22-foot boat I rotated the electric motor's shaft 180 degrees (see photograph on page 42). I can reach the aft-facing handle in my small jonboat from the bow seat; and it's no problem to reach the handle facing aft on the big boat's transom.

My small electric motor was not designed for heavy duty in salt water. Even so, it has held up well for eight summers.

Recently I bought a Minn Kota RT36/S electric motor with a stainless steel shaft and other parts; it promises long service in the salt. It has a KotaStow bracket that allows me to raise the motor halfway— enough to have it out of the water when the boat is on plane as we run back for another drift. Even so, I always attach a safety rope to the electric in case the transom screws work loose.

Guide Perry Munro, above, of Wolfville, Nova Scotia, mounts his electric motor on the transom of his 14-foot Whaler. This gives his anglers in the bow first shot at the water. Bow-mounted electrics give the *guide* first shot.

A Small Backup Motor   53

Several friends have small backup motors on the transom of their fishing boats. One buddy had five breakdowns of his old inboard-outboard motor one summer, but he has a 15 hp Mercury outboard on a transom-mounted bracket he can lower, and, while a lot slower than his main power plant, it does get him home. On one of those trips, I began to think about a get-home motor for my 22-foot hull.

The transom on my 22-foot Angler hull is wide enough to accommodate a small outboard alongside the 175 hp Johnson that provides the main power. After carefully measuring for width and shaft length, I decided on a 15 hp, 4-cycle Suzuki long-shaft motor. ("Long shaft" is a relative term—on a big engine, a long shaft is 25 inches, but a long shaft on a small motor is 20 inches.) Luckily, I did not need an outboard motor bracket that must be lowered to use the motor; I simply tilt it down and start it.

Since the Suzuki is a 4-cycle engine, it uses fuel from the main tank; it does not need to have oil mixed with its gas. A water-separator filter with two inputs and two outputs feeds both engines. One input is plugged, but both outputs are used. The starter's electric cables are routed to the battery compartment and secured to the main engine's steering and supply lines with cable ties, a neat installation.

A device is available that connects two motors of different sizes; either one can be tilted up and the other one steered from the helm. I may make one myself.

The small motor has a still further use—it is smoke free and quiet, so I use it for flounder trolling, as I once did with the electric motors mentioned previously.

And, should the big motor let me down, I can still get back to the dock!

Making a New Pedestal Seat Base   54

When the bolts loosened that held the pedestal seats on my 1974 20-foot Mako, I was afraid a seat might pull loose on acceleration and injure someone. The wood backer plate for the seat screws under the fiberglass deck had rotted because of water intrusion, but the wood was between two molded-in bait tanks in the afterdeck and an underdeck gas tank forward and therefore inaccessible. To get to the rotten wood, I would have had to remove the console and the cover plate under it and then remove the gas tank—either is a lot of work.

Instead, with considerable help from Jack Stovall, we made a new base from two pieces of ⁵⁄₄-inch teak, glued edge-to-edge to make a piece that was wide enough and long enough to accommodate the two pedestal seats. Then, the top and corners of the teak board were rounded with a router. Next, fifty ³⁄₄-inch-diameter holes were drilled about ¹⁄₂ inch deep with a sharp Forstner bit to accommodate fifty ³⁄₄-inch-diameter plugs made from a piece of scrap teak. Smaller holes were drilled through the center of the bottom of the ³⁄₄-inch holes for stainless steel screws that would anchor the seat base to, and through, the fiberglass deck.

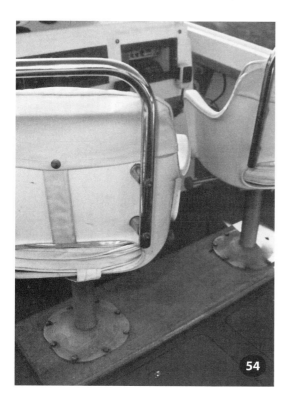

54

A pencil line was drawn around the completed seat base on the boat deck so it would be easy to quickly put the base in place when epoxy was applied to the deck and the bottom surface of the base.

West System two-part clear epoxy was applied to the deck and bottom of the base, the base lined up with the penciled lines, and fifty screws pulled the base down tight. Once the epoxy set up, the screw-covering plugs were painted with epoxy and tapped in to cover the screw heads, leaving ⅛ inch or so of each wood plug sticking up above the teak base. Once the epoxy applied to the plugs set up, the plugs were sanded off flush for a neat job.

Next, the seat bases were lag-screwed

into the new teak base, and the seat pedestals secured to the bases.

The installation was sturdy and secure. The seats had no play in them, even with a 200-pound man trying to rock them back and forth. One additional advantage was the extra 1¼ inch of seat height that gave the captain better visibility over the console.

Marine Radio Installations   55

A gradual shift from CB (citizens band) radios to VHF (very high frequency) sets has helped us pass on fishing hot spots to our buddies. There were so many CB sets in autos and trucks that airwaves became too crowded for reliable communications, so inshore anglers left CB for VHF.

During the transition from CB to VHF, I installed one of each type radio in the glove compartment of my 20-foot Mako. I cut away part of the back wall of the glove compartment for wiring and removed the entire unit for winter storage. One radio had its speaker in the bottom of the set, so it was mounted to the top of the compartment. Since the other radio's speaker was in the top of the set, it was mounted to the bottom of the compartment, so each one would broadcast toward the center of the compartment. (The glove compartment shows in the photograph at left.)

My present VHF radio is installed through the bulkhead near the steering wheel on my 22-foot walk-around cuddy hull. It has a water-resistant front panel, and all the controls are on the front of the set. Woe is me if I have a problem with the set since it is weatherproofed (read: permanently caulked in) with 3M 5200 Marine Adhesive Sealant.

My criteria for a VHF radio for the boat included a front panel speaker (a large remote extension speaker gives better reception), a numeric keypad so I could immediately change channels, and a front panel microphone plug. Since most of the anglers in our area have switched to VHF, some of the locals have returned to CB radios for a modicum of security. But, the really good stuff is communicated via cell phones!

The small triangular bulkhead just inside the cabin door on the right side in the 22-foot Angler was just large enough to mount a marine version of an AM/FM cassette-tape radio. Luckily, the boat's wiring center is just behind that bulkhead. Speakers for this radio are flush mounted on the bulkheads on either side of the steering station.

A 6-foot VHF antenna with a lift-and-lay mount is affixed to the starboard gunwale. The AM/FM radio's antenna wire is connected to a bolt inside the cabin on the underside of a bow rail bracket; music, news, and weather update reception is great!

Angler-boaters may want to consider switching to digital select calling (DSC) radios, which have the "potential to save many lives within a few years," according to BoatU.S. Once the DSC radio is installed, has a registered ID number, and is connected to a GPS (global positioning system) or loran unit, the unit can be used for pri-

vate ship-to-ship calls (like a cell phone), and Mayday distress calls (starting in 2002 to 2006) may be monitored by the U.S. Coast Guard, commercial ships, or both as a part of the Global Maritime Distress and Safety System (GMDSS). Contact your local marine supply store for more information as this new system comes into wider use.

Locker Cover Repairs 56

Boat manufacturers often use plywood or end-grain balsa wood as stiffeners under locker or baitwell covers, especially those on which people can walk.

My 1974 Mako hull had two bait tanks built under the deck behind the seats. The tanks' removable covers were reinforced with small pieces of balsa wood, encapsulated with another layer of fiberglass on the underside. After the hull was about fifteen years old, the covers had taken quite a beating from constant walking, running—even jumping. The fiberglass developed cracks on the underside of the covers. This allowed moisture to seep into the balsa wood, which became mushy and ruined as a stiffener. I took out all the balsa and replaced it with $\frac{1}{2}$-inch marine plywood, which was painted with several coats of West System epoxy, then it was laminated together with the top and bottom layers of fiberglass as it had been originally.

The same thing has happened to my latest hull, the 22-foot Horizon by Angler. Two lockers with hinged covers are handy places to store things or can even be made into baitwells. But, they are in high traffic areas of the boat and are also a handy place to jump on when getting aboard.

The covers were stiffened with plywood, but the constant pounding from 200-pounds-plus anglers soon cracked the fiberglass encapsulation around the ³/₈-inch plywood. In this case, the fix was simpler. The ³/₈-inch plywood was replaced with stronger ³/₄-inch marine plywood. West System epoxy was painted on the plywood (two coats). When the epoxy cured, the new plywood was covered with fiberglass cloth, which was wetted with two coats of epoxy. After the epoxy cured, the encapsulated wood was painted with exterior white latex. White gelcoat would have been another overcoat option.

Many other cracks or fissures on boats can be repaired in similar fashion. If in doubt about how to proceed, contact your local boating supply store for directions and materials.

The underside of the locker cover after the epoxy cured.

Can and Cup Holders 57

Spilled beverages in the boat can make a sticky mess, sometimes bad enough to draw flies.

Holders can be quickly made in the home shop to accommodate beverages in can coolers, mugs, or "sippers."

Schedule 40 PVC pipe of the proper inside diameter (ID) is one option, though a bit heavy. Another possibility is 4-inch ID thin-wall sewer pipe. I made a simple holder from a 4½-inch length of new, unperforated sewer drain-field pipe, and an end cap and attached it to the top of the console on my 22-foot walk-around cuddy cabin hull with double-sided foam mounting tape. It is large enough to hold any mug or can cooler I use. It holds beverages in place in rough seas, though any container with an open top is bound to slosh out some liquid in a sloppy seaway.

Cup holders can also be made from sheet polyethylene or from woods like teak or mahogany, which survive in the marine environment. An ingenious bulkhead-mount cup holder I saw in a catalog was made of three pieces of wood and folds up when not in use.

One Angler's Marine Electronics 58

My friend Marty Jester stared at me in disbelief when I explained at lunch one day how I had wired the electronics on the 16-foot Boston Whaler I had 36 years ago.

"I had a CB radio, a flasher depth-finder,

and navigation lights," I told Marty. "I ran two lengths of 4-gauge cable from the engine through the Whaler's tunnel to the battery that was wedged under the front seat." So far, so good.

"Then, I took some brown lamp cord (Marty stopped his sandwich halfway to his mouth) and ran it from the battery to the switches on the console (he began to choke), and hooked up the radio and depthfinder with those little blue things (choke, choke) you squeeze together to connect wires."

I had the feeling that he disapproved. Marty, who has installed marine electronics and electrical equipment since 1973 on every kind of watercraft from Exxon

Marty Jester at the console of a 36-foot Stamas.

tankers to fishing boats, was frowning. "Was that a no-no?" I asked. "A big no-no," he replied.

Lamp cord is not an approved wire for marine use. Marty recommends marine-grade tinned wire. "You should also use the right crimping tool and connectors," he said. "And, wire connections exposed to the weather or bilges should be covered with heat-shrink tubing that has a sealer incorporated."

While I got away with my shade-tree mechanic's marginal practices for several years, I did have a lot of potentially troublesome electronic equipment failures on my older boats that were caused by corroded connections.

I asked Marty about the most common electrical problems he is called upon to fix.

"Undersized wiring is one of the biggest problems we've had over the years," Marty said. "When you start adding accessories like washdown pumps, radios, spotlights, and other goodies, the wiring often won't carry the load. You don't get proper performance, and you've shortened the life span of your equipment."

I explained that on my previous 20-foot Mako hull, I gathered up all the loose wires under the console and tied them to the steering cable to get them out of the way.

"That does provide some strain relief," Marty said, "wiring shouldn't hang by its connectors." The problem reappears when a new steering cable is installed and the wires are cut loose and not reattached.

On my Mako, I noticed the compass was affected by the nearby VHF radio's speaker magnet on a trial placement. I had to move the radio to the opposite side of the console to avoid magnetic interference.

Marty just installed a complete electronics package on a 36-foot Stamas and offered to show it to me when we finished lunch. What planning must be done before cutting a lot of holes in a new boat's command center?

"We work with owners to decide what their final goals are," Marty said. "We leave room for future installations, make sure everything is within reach of the helm, that nothing obstructs the operator's view. We make doubly sure there is room behind the panel for surface mounted units."

What about the average boater who wants to install his or her own electronics? I installed the electronics on all my boats, first the 16-foot Whaler, then a 20-foot Mako, and lately on my 22-foot walk-around cuddy hull. As I upgraded boats, I also added more gear and equipment.

My 1964 Whaler had Marty's minimum recommended electronic package for anglers—lighting package, compass, depthfinder, and CB radio. The compass and depth-finder, I learned in the U.S. Power Squadrons' Basic and Advanced Piloting courses, can be used in combination with charts to estimate your approximate location. The radio is backup in case all else fails.

Our 1974 Mako had a compass, depthfinder, two radios (CB and VHF), loran, one bilge pump, two batteries with a switch, and lots of neat switches and gauges. Wiring was a bit messy, but I knew where it all was, and it never let me down. The loose wires

were gathered together and secured to the steering cable. The boat served me well for eighteen years.

To keep various antennae to a minimum so I could cast lures 360 degrees around the boat, I substituted a 40-inch piece of ¼-inch-diameter stainless steel rod for the loran antenna that usually screws into the end of the bottle-shaped preamplifier at the end of the long cable. I read in *Salt Water Sportsman* magazine that someone used a bow rail as a substitute loran antenna, so I tried that. It didn't work for me. The 40-inch-long rod worked. I hid it under the gunwale above the Mako's rod pocket. Later, I installed my makeshift loran antenna horizontally in the 22-foot Angler's cabin. These installations are not factory recommended. One should use an antenna matched to the electronic instrument. But, the combination worked for me for sixteen years.

Our recent 22-foot Angler hull has the same complement of electronics, less a CB radio, but I added a cell phone and an AM/FM radio with a tape deck. Wiring is neatly connected to a wiring bus behind the instrument panel and tied together to provide strain relief. Any wiring connections I made have been soldered and covered with shrink tubing, which adds to my confidence but would run up labor costs on a yard installation. The new Johnson 175 Ficht engine takes a lot of juice, so I use two MCA-1,000-rated batteries (1,000 marine cranking amps). The battery switch is set on "both" when the boat is in use. With the previous smaller batteries, starting the engine took power away from the depth-finder, cell phone, and loran, so they had to restart themselves with a "beep" or two.

My loran became somewhat forgetful. When it said I was at waypoint 11 (our dock), I was still 5 miles down the creek. That is not a great way to find your way home in the fog. I later found that the antenna plug was corroded and needed a little TLC in the form of cleaning, plus some resoldering inside the unit, to give me back the excellent signal-to-noise ratio (SNR) I had when the unit was new.

"Get a GPS," Marty said. "I don't know of a single manufacturer who is still making loran units—and GPS prices are coming down every day." The global positioning system (GPS), as most people know, had a built-in "dithering," or inaccuracy, of 100 meters (over 300 feet) until recently, so our enemies couldn't use the space satellite-based system against us. Seems to me that an atomic bomb landing 300 feet from a target could still do a fair amount of damage. An add-on unit called "DGPS" can improve the accuracy of the GPS. Recently, the dithering was removed from the GPS system; now accuracy is about 30 meters or less and is almost pinpoint with DGPS.

Recent improvements in GPS technology have made that system even more accurate, and as time goes on, even more incredible advances will be made.

Some of the newest goodies for marine anglers include computer programs like those from MapTech (available from marine supply stores) that can be loaded into a laptop computer (or a desktop if you have enough space and 110-volt AC power), and

Lowrance X70A depth-finder on the left with a new Lowrance GlobalMap 1600 on the boat console.

continually display your position on the computer's screen, plus tide and current data. Your computer is connected to the GPS to allow them to communicate together. Using this technology, you can display a navigation chart side-by-side with an aerial photograph of the same area.

For anglers who have great fishing spots stored on their old loran units, a computer program to convert loran TDs to GPS-Lat/Lon positions is called Positioning Aid 2.1a. A download is available for free from the Web site of the U.S. Coast Guard Research and Development Center.

So, I bought a Lowrance GlobalMap 1600 GPS. It has a reasonably large screen (4 inches square), and maps of my home area are already installed. In addition, I can load other maps and even offshore wrecks into the unit from a CD-ROM that fits my computer. The GlobalMap 1600 has a magnet on the back of its hockey-puck size antenna so it will adhere to the top of my car, and road maps can be loaded so we can tell where we are when traveling. An extra power cord for the car is the only accessory we need. The 1600's mounting bracket is affixed to the boat on a ¼-inch stud with a stainless steel wing nut so the GPS mounting bracket can easily be moved to a car. To store the lengthy antenna cable, I wound it on a plastic 16 mm motion picture film reel and attached the antenna to the reel.

The long cable to the GPS antenna is wound on an old plastic 16 mm film reel for easy portability and less mess on the boat's console.

Other useful electronic accessories include, but are not limited to, radar, autopilot, a laptop computer that contains navigation software and with the right connections shows your location on color charts, even seawater temperature. Satellite television may be gilding the lily on a small boat, but owners of larger craft may want

the convenience in addition to single-sideband (SSB) radio and other goodies. Scan the latest catalogs for updated technology.

Thirty-six years ago I was as happy as a Lab puppy with my minimal electronic accessories. Today, I have the bare minimum of gear for the way I fish, and I consider everything necessary. That's progress.

Quick Tips for Anglers

59 A yardstick can be applied to a cooler or the fishing boat in a handy place, but the sun will bleach out the ink over time. If you can find one, a yardstick printed on plastic sheeting with an adhesive backing is ideal. I bought two at a fishing show for $1 each and sliced them lengthwise to remove the advertising. The one on top of my starboard gunwale has been there since 1992 and still hasn't faded.

60 In addition to the ruler on the gunwale, other measuring devices on the cooler are an L-shaped board with a yardstick

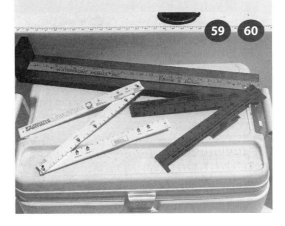

attached (the fish's nose goes against the upright board for accuracy), a Florida Lawstick from *Florida Sportsman* magazine, and a free folding fish and crab ruler from the Maryland Department of Natural Resources. The Igloo cooler also has a ruler molded into its top.

61 Sooner or later, you will find mold, oil residue, or both in your boat's bilge. Boating supply stores sell environmentally safe cleaners to use in the bilge. Some boaters allow a little fresh water and dish detergent to slosh around in the bilge if it can be safely drained later. Don't even think about draining oil overboard!

62 Use your flasher-type depth-sounder to indicate hard or soft bottom. Generally, fish will be over hard bottom, and uneven or oyster-shell bottom is often the best. First, turn down the sensitivity until you get only one bottom indication, with no "doubling." (Doubling occurs when the sensitivity is too high, and when the known depth is 30 feet—doubling will give two readings, one at 30 and another at 60 feet. This does not work with the new automatic LCD finders.) With a single reading at 30 feet and the sensitivity turned back to show one reading over soft bottom, you will get doubling when the boat moves over hard bottom. The bottom reading will be jagged, composed of different-width lines, or blips, when showing uneven or oyster-shell bottom.

63 Flats boats can be equipped with an upside-down, U-shaped leaning post of stainless steel pipe socketed into the front deck to give the angler something to lean against when tired and something to grab when tossed around by a wake.

64 On my Angler walk-around cuddy, there is a step-down that is often unnoticed by guests or yours truly. To call attention to this step-down, I made my own "safety stripe" tape by applying a strip of yellow waterproof tape the width of the step, then adding squares of black waterproof electrician's tape on top of the yellow strip.

65 Consider carrying an extra battery as a backup. I often bring along a spare and use it to power my electric trolling motor if I plan to use it a lot. I lift it onto the dock to recharge it, using an auto battery charger plugged into a GFCI (ground fault circuit interrupter) breaker-protected outlet.

66 I also carry a 4-gauge copper wire jumper cable set in a plastic storage container with a lid for backup in the boat. It is long enough to reach from my two battery compartments to the battery in the next boat if both of my batteries are down. It has happened.

67 If your outboard motor's oil tank is out of sight, install a dash-mounted oil level gauge so you can keep an eye on it. And, keep an extra gallon of outboard oil aboard just in case.

68 Carry a tool kit and include fuses for your motor and dash.

DOCKS, TRAILERING, AND ANCHORING

Docks

Parallel Boat Docking 69

In narrow waterways like canals, docks perpendicular to the shoreline are not practical, so I attached a parallel dock to the wooden bulkhead like a shelf. Two stainless steel pipe brackets held my 16-foot Boston Whaler and later a 20-foot Mako secure. Since relatively deep water was available right up to the bulkhead, my parallel-docked boats were afloat even at low tides.

First, a heavy-duty "shelf" was attached parallel to the wooden bulkhead. The pilings were about 8 feet apart, so a span of three pilings gave me three "shelf" braces at 8-foot intervals. Since the decking boards

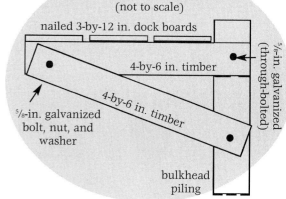

End view of parallel dock supports
(not to scale)

nailed 3-by-12 in. dock boards

4-by-6 in. timber

4-by-6 in. timber

$\frac{5}{8}$-in. galvanized
bolt, nut, and
washer

$\frac{5}{8}$-in. galvanized
(through-bolted)

bulkhead
piling

overhung each end brace 2 feet or so, I had about a 20-foot dock.

Dock supports were made from creosoted 4-by-6-inch timbers bolted together and to the pilings with $\frac{5}{8}$-inch galvanized bolts, nuts, and washers.

69

The author with the catch of the day in his parallel-docked Boston Whaler.

Recently, treated lumber for docks and piers has replaced creosoted lumber, which is an ecological no-no here on the Chesapeake Bay. *Check local regulations in your area.*

Once the three dock supports were bolted to the pilings with their top surfaces level, I nailed 3-by-12-inch dressed lumber on top of the supports as decking.

I had two stainless steel pipe-support brackets fabricated, one to be bolted to each end of the dock to secure the Whaler at bow and stern. Each bracket was made of three 12-inch-square pieces of ¼-inch-thick stainless steel plate. A crosspiece of ½-inch-round stainless pipe stock was welded to a 6-inch piece of 1¼-inch ID pipe held between the upright plates so it would pivot. A ⁵⁄₁₆-inch hole was drilled vertically through the pivoting pipe for a ¼-inch bolt. Holes were drilled in each corner of the bottom plates of the brackets for ⅝-inch bolts to fasten them to the dock.

Both standoff pipes were of 1-inch ID stainless steel. The stern pipe was long enough to reach from the starboard stern lifting eye on the Whaler to 6 inches beyond the shoreside bracket when the boat was pushed off 24 inches from the dock. The bow pipe reached from the shoreside bracket to the boat's bow cleat.

Holes were then drilled in the standoff pipes for near (12 inches from the dock) and far (24 inches from the dock) boat locations. The ¼-inch bolt was simply slipped through the captive pipe in each bracket and through the 1-inch standoff pipe at the location where the boat would be secured. Holes were drilled in the outboard end of

each standoff for galvanized eyebolts. Large galvanized snaps were spliced to each eyebolt with ½-inch nylon rope.

When the Whaler was docked, the ends of each standoff pipe were snapped to the Whaler's bow and stern. Pipes were slipped through the dock brackets until the boat was 24 inches away from the dock. Then the ¼-inch bolts were placed through the standoff and dock bracket to secure.

To draw the boat close enough to the dock to get aboard, the ¼-inch bolts were removed and the pipes slipped back to the second bolt holes and secured with the ¼-inch bolts. The pivoting 1¼-inch ID pipe inside the steel bracket allowed the boat to rise and fall with the tide.

When the 20-foot Mako replaced the Whaler (see photo on page 56), the pipe brackets had to be moved farther apart, making it necessary to mount the brackets on the wooden bulkhead. The bow snap was also modified to fit the Mako. Docking or undocking was a snap—or two.

Stainless Steel Bracket
(not to scale)

sliding pipe (length to suit)

near dock bolt position

pivot pin

weld

away from dock bolt position

eyebolt and rope spliced to snap to secure boat

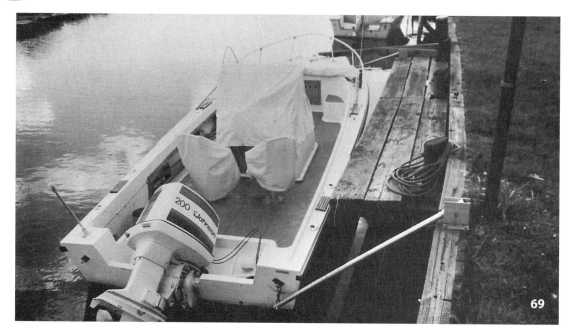

The 20-foot Mako parallel-docked.

Boat Slip Deicer 70

Several deicers are available in boat supply catalogs, including propeller and bubbler systems that run on house current. All are efficient, but my neighbor Bob Mason made up his own deicer from surplus parts gathered up around his shop, and it works great!

Retired engineer Bob is a tinkerer who never throws anything away. So, he has plenty of parts from just about everything to make just about anything.

To protect his sailboat from winter ice at his dock, he came up with an ingenious solution. An air-conditioning compressor from an old Dodge was mated to a 1-horsepower, 220-volt electric motor and mounted on a board. The motor is controlled by a thermostat set below freezing that operates a low voltage power-handling relay. The rig sits outside his house under a plastic tub.

Instead of running the power line to the dock with an associated electric power loss, he pumps the air through the underground water supply pipe from the house to the dock. There, compressed air goes to a weighted perforated pipe lying on the bottom around his boat. A hard freeze closes the thermostat, which powers the compressor that pumps air to the perforated pipe around the sailboat hull. Bubbles circulate warmer bottom water upward to melt ice forming around the boat.

Bob used a regular bubbler hose made for the purpose around his boat. One could also try a vinyl garden soaker hose and tie heavy fishing sinkers every foot along it to keep it from floating.

71

Temporary Boat Dock   71

I saw this clever temporary boat dock on a lake in New Brunswick, Canada. It seemed like a great solution to winter ice damage and in fact is the most common kind of boat dock used there. Just pull the dock up on dry land in late fall, then reposition it after ice-out in the spring.

A pair of wheels on an axle from a wrecked vehicle can be mounted on a U-shaped bracket and bolted to the end of the "dock" to provide mobility. Pipes driven into the ground at water's edge are joined by a crossbar to support the beach end of the dock. A sloping ramp secured to the driven pipes provides access across beach mud.

Dockline Pulley to Help Boarding   72

A ½-inch-capacity galvanized pulley (top arrow in photograph, page 58) with a flat mounting surface was secured with two 5-inch-long galvanized lag bolts to the starboard mooring piling in a vertical position. This allows the portside stern of my 22-foot outboard hull to be pulled close enough to the dock for easy boarding.

The starboard stern mooring line was attached to the boat's stern cleat and threaded through the pulley, then secured at its end to a cleat on the dock piling.

The boat can be secured in its moored position by pulling the starboard line until the boat is centered in its space, then the

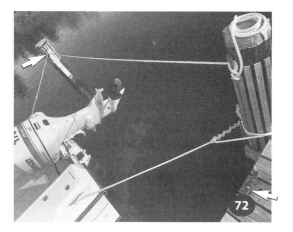

A possible way to build such a ramp would include 2-by-6-inch or 2-by-8-inch treated lumber for side rails, large-diameter galvanized pipe screwed into pipe flanges at both ends, and pieces of PVC pipe slipped over the galvanized pipe for rollers. You will need some way of anchoring the ramp for high water conditions.

The leaning position of the angler in the photo indicates he should get some help so he doesn't hurt his back!

line is secured to the cleat on the dock piling. When the boat needs to be next to the dock for boarding, the line on the piling cleat is loosened and enough slack is allowed so the boat comes close to, but does not touch, the dock. The portside stern dockline is wrapped around a cleat fastened to the dock boards (bottom arrow in photograph above) to restrain it close to the dock.

In areas of high winds or long fetches across big waters, I would not recommend this system—especially for boats much over 20 feet!

C. BOYD PFEIFFER

Small Boat Roller Ramp   73

This novel boat conveyor was used to move boats around a dam in Louisiana. It may have been made commercially.

It struck me that a similar rig could be made to beach small boats on lakes or even tidal waters if the tide range is not too great—or if the beach doesn't have a steep slope.

Snook Lights for Stripers   74

Florida anglers often fish after dark under "snook lights" at the ends of docks. Lights directed into the water attract baitfish or shrimp. Snook congregate under the lights to feed.

In Chesapeake Bay waters, lights shined downward from the end of a dock will attract baitfish, which in turn entice striped bass.

Get an electrician to rig a snook light on your dock, and make sure the electrical outlet is ground fault circuit interrupter (GFCI) protected so no one gets an electric shock.

The light must shine down into the water where it is fairly deep, perhaps 4 to 6 feet at the end of the dock. Leave it on from just after dark for about three hours every night, when the snook feed in Florida, or from May to October on Chesapeake Bay.

This same system may be used anywhere gamefish feed on light-attracted baitfish at night.

Flies or small lures that mimic baitfish cast into the breaking fish under the light will almost always result in strikes. Also, check out the edge of the light—many gamefish wait in the dark to ambush baitfish blinded by the light.

Tide Indicator   75

Ed Schartner made this tide gauge and indicator in the 1960s, and I told him he should have patented the ingenious device.

The lower pipe is white PVC, and the upper clear pipe fits into the lower pipe via a machined adapter. The bottom is open to allow water to raise a weighted float. The top is open so air isn't trapped inside. The lower end of the bottom pipe that is submerged in tidal waters most of the time is coated with an antifouling paint to ward off barnacles and oysters.

Connecting the bottom weight-float and the upper (white) tide-height indicator is a stainless steel rod. The dark button (see arrow in photograph below) inside the upper indicator is spring-loaded to provide friction against the interior of the clear tube so it will pop up when the tide starts to ebb; it disappears into the white indicator when

the tide is rising. The dark button is captive in the white indicator so it will only move upward three-quarters of its length. Some details need to be worked out by the skilled person who wants to build one of these units. I've never seen one on the market.

The unit is mounted high enough on the dock so it can be seen from the house. Two exterior sliding white rings on the clear pipe indicate the high-low range of tides. The entire unit is bracketed to the dock with U-bolts to adjust for tidal ranges.

When the dark button can be seen, it tells the boater the tide is ebbing, and the shallow creek entrance will soon be too shoal for navigation. When the button is hidden inside the upper white indicator, the tide is flooding.

Annual maintenance consists of removing the unit so winter ice won't destroy it, as well as periodic cleaning.

Rope and Pulley Tie-Out   76

One of the simplest ways to tie out a small boat is to drive a stake or pipe in the bottom where there is enough water to float the craft and add a pulley near the top of it facing the shore.

A continuous loop of rope between the pulley and shore with a short dropper attached to the bow of the boat, and another dropper attached to the stern, makes it easy to bring the boat in.

This can be a temporary rig while a per-

76

manent dock is being built or a semiperma-
nent rig in protected waters. It is not recommended for open waters with a long
fetch across them where high winds can
build high seas and do considerable
damage.

Boat Dock Fishing Bench 77

In the photograph, the author installs PVC
pipe rod holders on his dock bench with a
cordless drill (safety first!) and stainless
steel square-drive screws.

The bench is made from treated lumber
in three sizes: 2-by-6-inch uprights and
legs, a 2-by-4-inch "box" frame to support

the seat and tie in with the legs, and 1-by-
6-inch seat and seatback. Galvanized 16-
penny nails tied the box frame and legs together. Galvanized roofing nails secured
the seat bottom and back to the box frame
and uprights.

Not visible in the center of the back of
the box frame is a galvanized eyebolt with a
diameter slightly larger than the pipe of a
table umbrella. The umbrella pipe slides
through the eyebolt, and its base is seated
in the 2-inch-by-4-inch block nailed to the
dock decking, visible just behind and under
the seat.

The bench is secured to the dock's decking boards with galvanized L-brackets and
stainless steel square-drive screws.

77

Trailering

Combined Jumper and Electric Winch Cable 78

An inexpensive homemade cable assembly can serve the angler as both a jumper cable and a boat trailer electric winch cable. It can be a car-to-car or boat-to-boat jumper cable: adding an electric winch plug and wire kit makes it a boat trailer electric winch cable that can be moved from one tow vehicle to another. The total length of my jumper-winch cable is 27 feet—21 feet for the jumper cables and a 6-foot power winch cable extension that is soldered to one end of the jumper cables.

I assembled my 21-foot jumper cables by soldering a black-handled battery cable clamp to each end of a 21-foot length of black insulated 4-gauge copper wire and soldering a red-handled clamp to each end of a 21-foot length of red insulated 4-gauge wire. All surfaces to be soldered were cleaned with steel wool, and after the wires were clamped firmly into the handles, the joints to be soldered were heated until the resin core solder melted and flowed into the junction. A wrap of electrical tape every foot or so along the entire length keeps the two cables together and tangle free.

My electric winch wiring kit consisted of a plug to fit into the power socket of the winch attached to a double cable of #6 copper wire. The black (–) negative conductor,

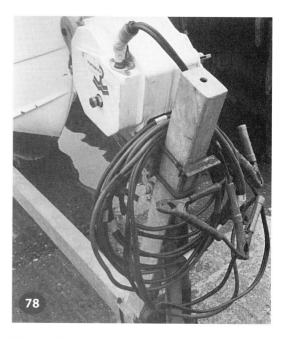

78

The combination cable after picking up the boat.

about 6 feet long, was soldered to the black battery clamp at one end of the jumper cable. *Observing proper polarity is important.* The longer of the two electric winch wires (red) was cut off even with the black one, and the small cans containing the winch circuit breakers were soldered between the red positive (+) power winch wire and the red jumper cable clamp.

Next, I checked the combined cable's polarity by connecting the polarized plug to the power winch and connecting the opposite end of the jumper cables to a 12-volt car battery, positive (red) clamp to positive (+) battery terminal and negative (black) clamp to the negative (–) battery terminal. With the winch switched on, the cable wound properly over the top of the drum.

In use, the trailer is backed into the

launching ramp before the jumper/winch cable is hooked up. After the power cable plug is inserted into the winch receptacle, the jumper-winch cables are extended on the ground to the front of the tow vehicle.

⚠ ***It is very important*** **to keep the red and black unused jumper cable clamps near the back of the vehicle separated by clamping one of them to the insulated cover of the opposite wire. Don't let the rear red clamp touch the car!**

After you raise the car's hood, attach the red clamp to the positive (+) post of the car's battery. Then, as recommended by auto safety experts, the black cable clamp is attached to the auto's metal bumper or frame at some distance from the battery to prevent sparks that could result in injury from an exploding battery.

The red (positive) clamp goes to the (+) battery terminal first and the black (-) clamp is secured to the metal bumper last for safety.

Combination Trailer Dolly and Spare Tire 79

In 1987, I attended the Minnesota Inventor's Congress and saw this combination trailer dolly and spare tire. I thought it had great merit, but I didn't get the inventor's name. The idea may now be patented.

While I do not recommend copying a patented invention, it may now be available in boating catalogs.

Trailer Hookup Mirror   80

Backing the tow vehicle to your boat trailer tongue can be chancy if no one is around to guide you.

There are several trailer alignment devices on the market, including a pair of fiberglass rods, one each attached to the car and trailer. One could make such a set from old fishing rods.

But I found that a low-cost truck rearview mirror attached to the winch stand on my trailer serves the same purpose. Once I properly adjusted the mirror so I can see it on the trailer, either over my shoulder or in my station wagon's rearview mirror, I carefully back up until the trailer's hitch receiver is over the ball on the wagon's hitch.

The mounting bracket that came with the mirror was adapted to fit under the U-bolt that holds the trailer winch's bracket. Once the mirror was adjusted, the saltwater exposure soon rusted the mirror's ball-and-socket joint in place.

Launch Ramp Safety Chocks   81

Photographs of cars that were unintentionally launched along with boats make many anglers nervous at a steep ramp. They wonder if their tow vehicle's emergency brake will hold while their boat is launched or retrieved.

Many of us who trailer our boats regularly use a set of chocks behind the vehicle's rear wheels when launching or retrieving.

You often see utility workers use chocks when they park their trucks to work on telephone or power lines—even if the truck is on level ground! You can copy their chocks, or make your own. Their chocks usually have a short loop of rope attached for easy removal. This is impractical on a boat ramp because the chocks must be removed before retrieving the boat so the trailer doesn't run over them, negating the safety aspect of the chocks.

Chocks can be made from a 24-inch piece of 6-by-6-inch wood cut in half at a 45-

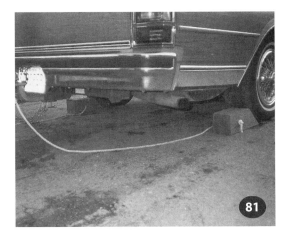

degree angle to make two equal pieces. Drill a ½-inch hole through each chock to accommodate ⅜-inch rope. Make the rope long enough to extend from one chock across the trailer hitch to the opposite chock but short enough so the chocks drag along out of reach of the trailer's wheels when retrieving the boat.

Turnbuckle-Up for Safety   82

A galvanized turnbuckle attached between my boat and trailer has provided me with an extra measure of safety while trailering and lets me remove my Powerwinch when the boat is in storage (a kit is available from Powerwinch to allow the unit to be easily removed).

First, I installed a ½-inch-diameter galvanized eyebolt on the trailer's winch stand upright. This eyebolt is the attachment point for one end of the turnbuckle.

My turnbuckle has a U-shaped clevis or shackle at each end and is a minimum of 13 inches long when the two ½-inch-diameter threaded screws are fully retracted. I replaced the two clevis or shackle pins in each end with ⅜-inch-diameter stainless cap screws that are 2 inches long. Nylok nuts were used on the cap screws so over-the-road vibration wouldn't loosen them.

The boat is winched tightly against the bow stop roller on the trailer and one clevis is bolted to the bow eye of the boat and the other to the eyebolt on the trailer. Then, I tighten the turnbuckle.

The extra measure of safety provided by

the turnbuckle is reassuring while trailering, but that is not the only reason I use it. Not only is my Powerwinch out of the weather during the winter, but also it is locked up out of sight when the boat is unattended at a ramp or motel. An extra measure of safety should be used: attach a piece of chain to the boat's bow eye and wrap it around the trailer's tongue directly below the eye. Fasten together with a clevis.

Trailer Walkboard   83

Adding a walkboard to a boat trailer can make the boat loading process safer and easier.

The walkboard for my Mako's trailer was a piece of 1-inch-by-12-inch pine shelving 8 feet long that matched the flat areas on the trailer cross-braces and spanned four of them. This allowed me to climb onto the board at the tongue end of the trailer and kept my feet dry when the wheel hubs were just out of the water.

Before I installed my walkboard, both

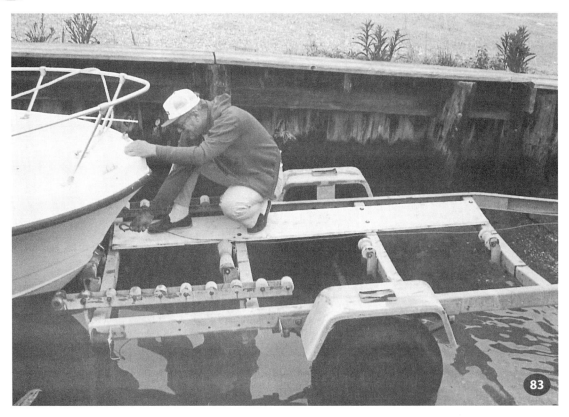

The author hooking up the Mako to load it on the trailer.

sides of it were rolled with white exterior latex paint. While the paint was wet, I sprinkled some dry sand on the upper side to give the walking surface some "tooth" to prevent me from slipping and falling.

To attach the walkboard to the trailer, I used ³⁄₈-inch-diameter stainless steel cap screws with washers on the upper side and stainless steel washers and stainless steel Nylok nuts on the underside.

Before walking to the rear of the trailer along the board, I locked the latch that keeps the trailer tongue from tilting. The hook end of the winch cable was in my hand as I walked along the board to hook it to the bow eye of the boat.

My walkboard was easy to install. The additional safety and the easier loading of my boat was worth the minimal effort and expense.

Some boat trailers will not accommodate a walkboard. Their cross-braces are made to accommodate a V-shaped hull. In that case, it may be possible to use an adhesive-backed skid guard safety tape with an abrasive surface on the trailer frame members that are relatively flat. The tape is available in hardware stores.

Jonboat Easy Loader   84

Loading an aluminum skiff or jonboat into the back of a pickup truck can be made easier by the simple installation of a boat trailer roller on the truck's tailgate.

Jack Stovall bolted a boat trailer roller purchased from a marine supply store a few inches from the end of the tailgate of his pickup. It is easy for him to lift one end of his (unloaded) 14-foot aluminum skiff onto the end of the tailgate, then lift the boat's opposite end and slide the boat as far as it will go toward the front of the truck's bed. There is plenty of room alongside the skiff for the outboard motor and tackle. Some states require that a red flag be tied to anything extending more than a foot or two behind the vehicle. Check your local laws about this.

Unloading the boat at your favorite fishing hole goes easier with two people, but a lone angler can still handle a lightweight skiff with the roller's help. Simply skid the boat to the shoreline, add motor and tackle, and push off. The procedure is reversed for picking up the skiff.

Trailer Loading Light   85

Anglers who pursue fish that bite best from late afternoon until after dark will, of course, return to the launching ramp and load their boats on trailers in the dark.

Many of these anglers install a 12-volt lamp under their electric winch to make loading the boat easier, and safer, after dark. These 12-volt lamps can be purchased in auto parts or marine supply stores.

It is simple to drill an appropriate hole in the winch stand near the power winch to mount the light and wire it directly to the power leads inside the winch. Make sure the light is not wired so it operates with the power winch switch, or the lamp will only come on when the winch is switched on. You want the lamp to be lighted when the power winch cord is plugged in to the winch.

This simple addition to a power winch can make the evening angler's life a little easier at boat loading time—and safer.

Tractor Hitch to Move Boats   86

Those who are lucky enough to have a farm tractor with a hydraulic three-point hitch can rig it to move their trailered boat around the yard for maintenance or to mow the area where it is normally parked.

You can buy a heavy-duty steel crossbar with several ¾-inch-diameter holes that attaches between the two lower lift arms. Check with your tractor dealer for the proper equipment. I fastened my crossbar ends with bolts and Nylok nuts for security, instead of using the standard ring clips that can come loose. I mounted one 2-inch trailer hitch ball and one 1⅞-inch hitch ball on the crossbar.

Since the crossbar can rotate and decouple the ball from the trailer receiver, I bolted a piece of 1½-inch-square bar stock between the crossbar and one three-point hitch lift arm as a stabilizer.

86

⚠ **Caution! Before attaching *any* three-point hitch implement, be sure any necessary weights are added and correctly distributed on the tractor for safe operation and stability! Front frame weights, wheel weights, and rear wheel weights are available. When lifting a heavy trailer, make sure you have adequate balance weights on the tractor. Use only implements and weights that are approved for that tractor. When moving boat trailers with this hitch system, lock the trailer ball in place. Also, use a low tractor gear and go slowly. On sloping ground, make sure you block trailer wheels securely before disconnecting the tractor so the trailer won't roll.**

⚠ *Never* **place your body or any body parts between the tractor and trailer or their parts at any time! Behave as if the equipment will hurt you if it can, because if you don't, it will!**

Trailering Tips

Before towing your boat on the open road, make a visual check of your rig:

87 Check all tire pressures with a gauge, including the spare. The maximum tire pressure is molded into the sidewall of the trailer's tires.

88 Check the trailer ball and safety chains. Chains should be crisscrossed under the trailer tongue to support the trailer in case you hit a bump and the hitch ball and coupler disconnect. Make sure the hitch coupler's locking lever is in the down position, the ball is locked to the coupler, and a pin or padlock is on the locking lever.

89 Make sure the winch cable is tight with the boat's bow against the stop. A safety chain should be connected between the boat's bow towing eye and the trailer to keep the boat from jumping over the winch stand. A strap or other tie-downs should be tight at the boat's stern to keep the boat and trailer together in case of a panic stop.

90 Raise the outboard motor or I/O lower unit to the towing position and lock it in place. Some motors use a separate motor brace for towing.

91 Make sure all the drain plugs are installed in your boat.

92 Prepare for launching before leaving home to avoid conflict at the launch ramp. Place all tackle, coolers, and other gear aboard the boat and attach lines to the bow and stern cleats for launching and docking. Secure everything so it won't blow out of the boat underway or fall overboard when launching.

93 Tongue weight is generally about 10 percent of the total loaded weight of the boat and trailer. Not enough weight on the tongue can cause the boat to fishtail at highway speeds and cause an accident. Too much weight on the tongue overloads the rear of the tow car and the hitch. Follow the trailer manufacturer's instructions.

94 Check the springs and axle for excess rust. I found several broken spring leaves on one of my trailers, which prompted me to replace springs, attaching bolts, axle, and bearings. One friend bent his trailer axle by crossing a ditch too soon. The axle was rusted almost through and could have let him down on the open road.

95 Check wheel bearings, and if they are worn, replace them before getting on the road. Add wheel bearing lubricators if you don't have them. Make a visual inspection of the grease in the clear plastic hub and add lubricant if necessary.

96 Check brake and directional signal lights before you leave home. Ask your partner to stand behind the trailer as you try directional signals and brakes and report if they are working. Replace burned-out bulbs, and make sure trailer plug contacts are free from corrosion.

97 If the trailer is equipped with brakes, check their adjustment according to the owner's manual, and make sure the breakaway lanyard is connected, with enough slack for tight turns.

98 License plate holders on boat trailers are subject to theft, wear, tear, and corrosion. Make sure the license plate is still in place.

99 Adjust the pressure in your tow vehicle's air-adjustable shock absorbers so that the boat trailer and tow vehicle are level.

100 Powerwinch sells a stud kit to replace the three bolts that hold its winch on the trailer winch stand. These studs fit the keyhole-shaped slots on the bottom of the winch. Once the studs are properly fitted to your winch stand, place the winch on the stand using the keyhole slots, and use a Nylok nut and bolt in the matching hole between stand and winch to make sure the winch doesn't slip. This allows you to remove the winch at boat ramps while you are out fishing and store it in the car trunk out of sight and also allows you to remove it for winter storage.

101 Consider replacing trailer bunks when necessary with treated 2-by-6-inch or 2-by-4-inch lumber. It will outlast the untreated boards. Teflon strips are better than carpet because they have less friction, but be sure to recess the nailheads.

102 When your boat is off the trailer, consider greasing or lightly oiling the trailer rollers for easier launching.

103 Trailer guide-ons didn't work for my 22-foot boat. No matter what I did, the boat was never centered on the trailer when retrieving.

My solution was to install a boat positioner made from 1-inch ID galvanized pipe nipple 10 inches long, threaded into a pipe flange and attached to one trailer fender with stainless steel bolts and Nylok nuts. A 12-inch piece of 1¼-inch ID PVC pipe fits over the galvanized pipe as a hull protector/roller, as shown below. While the boat is on the trailer in the water, a buddy stands on the boat's portside with a boat hook and a short line and adjusts the hull so it is about an inch from the PVC positioner. My solution may not be sanctioned by boat or trailer manufacturers, but it works for me.

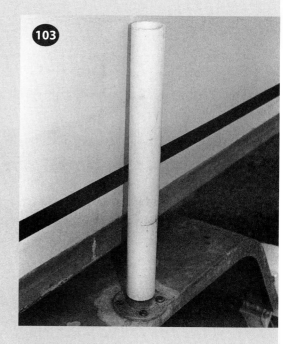

PVC boat positioner.

Be secure in the knowledge you have checked everything in your control. Drive defensively when towing—remember to add distance to the interval between you and the car ahead, because the extra weight of your towed rig adds to your stopping distance.

Anchoring

Anchoring for Anglers   104

In recent years, chumming for stripers, weakfish, and croaker has become popular on the Chesapeake Bay and for other fish in other places. But, if you want to see a disaster about to happen, watch the chumming fleet on a windy day. Anchors continually break loose and boats drift downwind toward others whose anchors are holding. It's like watching a train wreck about to happen. There is nothing you can do but watch and hope the drifters soon learn more about anchoring before they hurt someone.

I have used a 9-pound 8S Danforth anchor since 1974 on two boats: a 20-foot Mako center console outboard hull and lately a 22-foot walk-around cuddy outboard. On the Mako, I attached a sash weight about 6 feet above the anchor with a large galvanized snap. I didn't want to store a heavy, rusty chain. In moderate holding conditions, a sash weight snapped to the anchor rode can be a temporary solution. The sash weight lies on the bottom like a piece of chain above the anchor and supplies horizontal pull to dig the anchor's flukes into the bottom. I still use 150 feet of ¹⁄₂-inch nylon rope as the rode, but on the newer boat I have a 6-foot length of heavy galvanized chain attached to the 8S Danforth anchor.

I am always concerned about a fishing buddy going forward to pull anchor in

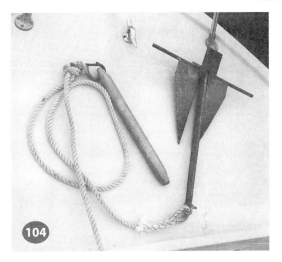

sloppy seas. So, I've tried several ways to pull anchor and stay amidships.

In the Florida Keys, a friend pulled anchor by starting his motor and idling off to one side until he was clear of the rode (he thought) and then motoring upwind. Unfortunately, he ran across the rode; it wrapped around his I/O lower unit and killed his motor. The boat swung around, stern to the wind. Waves came over the transom. We finally got the rode unwrapped, but that situation was doubly scary because the other fishing boats had left for the day and we were alone. I do not recommend this system!

A variation on that idea is often used offshore. A float ball with a large snap (available from most marine supply stores) is clipped over the anchor rode outboard of the bow cleat. The boat moves ahead until the anchor pulls out of the bottom. When the anchor rode has pulled all the way through the large snap ring, the anchor engages the ring. Then the floating anchor is retrieved safely aboard into the after cockpit. But, again, there is the possibility the rode can wrap around the propeller. Scary!

I use a variation on the last two systems. If it might be rough where I plan to fish, I get the anchor out of the bow compartment in calm water. I then tie off a suitable length of rode to the bow cleat. The anchor and a 5-to-1 scope of rode (150 feet of rode for a depth of 30 feet) are secured aft in the cockpit. Then, I snap a 20-foot length of "slider" line over the rode outboard of the bow rail and tie the other end to the after end of the bow rail at the cockpit. When setting or retrieving the anchor in rough water, no one needs to go forward. It takes two to retrieve the anchor with this system. One to run the boat ahead and to one side of the rode very slowly as the other person, safe in the aft cockpit, takes in line as the snap slides down the rode toward the anchor. When 20 feet or less of the "slider" line is in, the anchor rode is in the puller's hands.

⚠ **Communication *must* be good between the captain and the anchor-puller so the rode *never* gets near the propeller.**

You often see workboats anchored from the stern (not recommended for small boats). You will also notice the anchor rode is almost vertical! How do the crew members do that? They use a grappling hook-style anchor with five flukes flattened on the ends to dig into the bottom. A length of chain is sometimes added.

One version of the grappling anchor (shown at right), used by charter Capt. Mike

Haddaway of Bozman, Maryland, has a ring at the base of the anchor for a "trip line." Mike often fishes the Airplane Wreck in the mouth of the Chesapeake Bay's Choptank River. If he gets hung up in the wreck, no problem. His trip line has a float he can haul aboard and untoggle his anchor from the wreck.

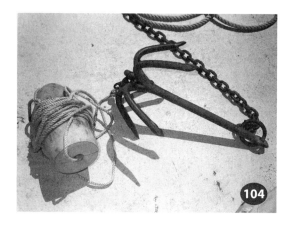

Several years ago, I took divers to the Airplane Wreck. This is not a place for amateur divers—jagged metal and fishhooks are everywhere. These chaps were pros. However, the line they rigged between our two boats caused my Danforth anchor to slip and toggle into the wreck. Since the divers used my anchor line as a vertical highway to the wreck, it was no problem for them to bring it up on their last dive. But the wreck is decorated with lots of anchors, so there must be another way. There is—a wreck anchor.

Consider two versions of wreck, or rockpile, anchors: rebar and aluminum-tined with a heavily weighted stock. The rebar and the aluminum-tined are designed to bend. Rebar anchors are made of $^3/_8$- or $^1/_2$-inch steel reinforcing rod, available from hardware stores. Four or five tines are welded together with a ring at the top for the anchor rode. A coat of paint keeps them from rusting and staining the boat. In use, the rebar anchor is toggled into a wreck or rock pile. If it won't come loose when it's time to leave, the tines can be pulled straight with boat power. Tines are easily rebent.

⚠ **Stay out of the way of a possibly breaking stretched line.**

Aluminum tines on the new 15-pound Mighty-Mite wreck-rock anchor are easily rebent, too. It has five $^5/_{16}$-inch aluminum bar stock tines, sharpened at the ends so they will hold in soft or hard bottom in addition to rocks and wrecks. The main difference in this anchor is that the tines and top ring are secured inside a heavily weighted $1^1/_2$-inch ID aluminum pipe. No chain is needed with this anchor, its maker says, because its stock is so heavy. This anchor is not tossed but is lowered slowly to the bottom. You don't want to toss it at a rock pile, either; since it is front-loaded, the stock will hit the rocks before the tines. The result is a lost anchor.

Those who chum the Chesapeake Bay Bridge pilings or rock piles want precise placement of chum, bait, or both in certain eddy currents. You will often see a combination of anchors used here: two Danforths or grappling anchors set in a V from the

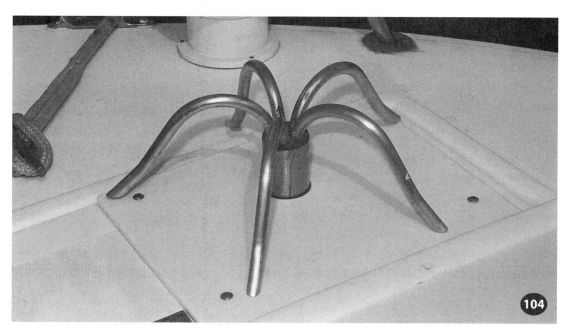

This Mighty-Mite anchor's stock fits down through a hole in the top of the anchor locker so the tines rest down on the top of the locker for safety.

bow and a rebar anchor attached to a stern cleat that is toggled into a rock pile aft. This allows precision placement of the boat by adjusting anchor rodes.

A small navy anchor (shown below) on a short rode (20 to 25 feet in my case) often comes in handy when fishing in shallow water. When you are drifting and casting surface plugs in 3 to 5 feet of water, a striped bass or bluefish might announce its presence by striking at the lure. A swirl or splash near the plug, and you want to stay in the area and check it out. Simply slide the small anchor overboard and secure its rode to a cleat. In calm water it will hold you in one place; in moderate winds, it might slide along the bottom, giving you the chance to make a few additional casts.

We've come a long way from the simple mushroom or cinder-block anchors that we used in small ponds and streams. Chesapeake Bay and other big waters can get rough. Rocks and wrecks often keep expensive anchors, so we look at cheaper alternatives. And high winds sometimes make me

wish I had bought a 13S Danforth anchor instead of the 8S that has served so well.

A Double Buoy for Precise Anchoring   105

Precise anchoring over a small wreck or obstruction that holds fish can be made easier with the simple addition of a small float on a 6-foot cord tied to your marker buoy.

Capt. Mike Murphy of Easton, Maryland, carries such a rig on his 25-foot charterboat. When he reaches a fishing spot like the Choptank River's Airplane Wreck, he drops his double buoy with enough weight at the end of the cord to keep it in place.

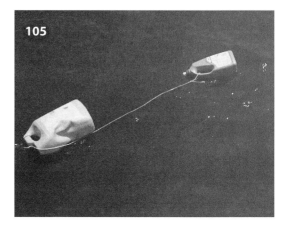

Then, he slowly circles his double buoy until he finds the wreck on his depthsounder. By this time, his double buoy has settled, and the smaller float on a short line off his buoy has swung around with the wind and current to show him which way his boat will lie at anchor. He simply motors upwind and upcurrent, as dictated by his double buoy, and then he anchors. It's funny, but new arrivals to fish the wreck often anchor next to his original buoy!

If you are lucky enough to get your double buoy directly on top of fish-holding structure, motor upwind or upcurrent of the double buoy, keeping the float and the buoy aligned, and drop anchor as far from the buoy as you need anchor rode scope to hold bottom. Then let out enough anchor rode to put you on top of the fish!

Quick-Release Anchoring Knot 106

Anglers who often encounter fish so large they must chase them with their boats need a fast way to either recover their anchor quickly or untie it and leave it in place. Some use a heavy-duty eye snap tied into the anchor rode that can be hooked to the boat's bow cleat or bow lifting eye.

Another solution to the quick-release problem is to use a two-loop system of attaching the anchor rode to the bow cleat. As illustrated at right, a loop is made in the rode and inserted through the bow cleat, and a second loop is formed in the next 2 feet or so of the rode and then inserted through the first loop. When the boat comes tight on the anchor rode, the second loop keeps the first loop from coming out of the bow cleat, assuming the doubled diameter of the rode's first loop neatly fits through the cleat's eye. Some trial-and-error fitting must be done so the first loop doesn't pull the second one through.

A float large enough to keep afloat in the

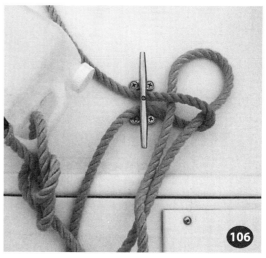

Quick-release anchoring knot.

current is secured to the bitter end of the rode.

To quickly untie the anchor rode, simply pull the second loop out of the first loop and toss the float overboard, chase the fish, then return to the float and retie your loops.

The loops can also be secured to the bow lifting eye, but that necessitates someone leaning out over the bow, which is not always safe or enjoyable in even a moderate sea.

In heavy seas, this system should not be used, since the two loops could bind in the cleat or bow eye under heavy pressure.

Anchoring Tips

Check boating supply catalogs or *Chapman Piloting: Seamanship and Small Boat Handling* for the latest anchor and rode recommendations.

107 Slow the drift of a small fishing boat by dragging a piece of heavy chain on the end of a rope. The photograph below shows such a drag anchor on the left, with a piece of rope just long enough so the chain won't tangle in the outboard motor's propeller when the boat moves from place to place. A new piece of chain is in the center. A homemade "coffee can" anchor is on the right, made by pouring concrete into a tin can and adding an eyebolt.

108 An anchor for rocky bottom can be made from an old steel plate used to anchor railroad rails to the wooden ties. Attach it to the anchor rode with a piece of chain for abrasion resistance.

⚠ **If you fish downstream of a dam that periodically releases a large flow of water, keep a knife handy to cut the anchor rode if you can't get the plate up when they blow the dam's warning horn!**

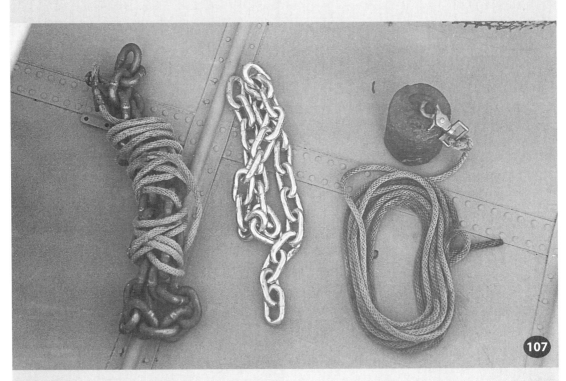

107

C. BOYD PFEIFFER

109 Make a wreck anchor with ³/₈-inch rebar reinforcement rod. Bend one 60-inch piece in half around a piece of pipe to make an eye and put it through an 18-inch-long piece of 1¹/₄-inch ID galvanized pipe. Cut two or three more pieces of rebar (as many as you can fit into the pipe), long enough to extend from the eye end of the pipe out the other end far enough to make anchor flukes the same length as the doubled piece. Pour enough epoxy into the pipe to grip the rebar pieces.

Bend the flukes with a 3- or 4-foot piece of pipe and keep it handy on board the boat to rebend the rebar after straightening it when pulling the stuck anchor off a wreck. Spray the anchor with aluminum paint.

110 Plastic buckets make good emergency sea anchors to keep your bow headed into the wind or slow your drift while fishing. Tie the bucket to the end of a 50-foot piece of line. If you want to drift broadside, make up a bridle from the bow to stern, then tie the sea anchor's line midway on the bridle with a bowline knot. A bucket towed astern will also slow your trolling speed, but keep the line away from the propeller!

111 For shallow-water casting, Sherman Baynard ties a small anchor to one end of a short rode and a 12-inch piece of wood closet rod to the other end as shown below. Luckily, one gunwale rod holder is exactly midships on his 17-foot Mako. He places the dowel in that rod

holder and drops anchor. His boat lies across the current, allowing one angler to cast from the bow and one from the stern.

112 As shown at right, a sailboater's cam cleat is mounted on the bow of an aluminum boat. The "coffee can" anchor's rode is temporarily suspended from the cam cleat. By pulling on the rode, the cam cleat opens so the angler can drop anchor. Then, the rode is allowed to ride against one side of the cam cleat as more line is fed out, closing the cleat.

C. BOYD PFEIFFER

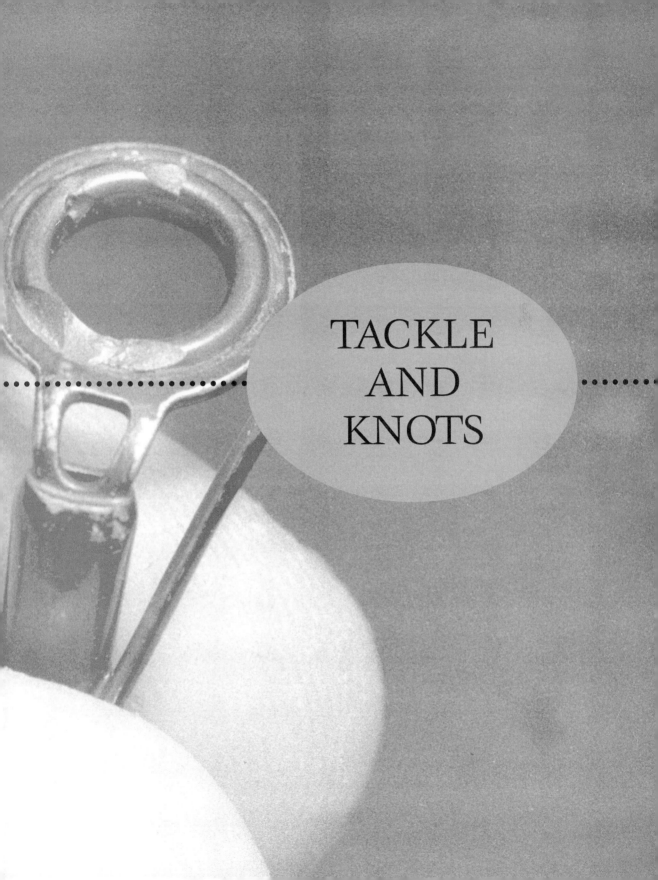

TACKLE AND KNOTS

Rods

Replacing Rod Guides and Tip-Tops   113

A broken rod guide or tip can easily be replaced by the home craftsperson. To replace a guide, gather up a few tools and materials: a rod guide that matches the broken one, thread (more on this later), scissors, single-edge razor blade, a two-part epoxy rod finish, and masking tape, plus a simple rod winding lathe like the one in Inexpensive Rod Winding Lathe, project 114.

Thread comes in many sizes and colors. Try to match the thread color on the remaining of your guide wraps on your rod. This is not always possible, but thread manufacturer Gudebrod lists thirty-three different colors, available from most tackle shops. Most thread manufacturers recommend using a color preserver on the thread after wrapping. If you use preserver, let it dry thoroughly before applying the epoxy rod finish. (The "N.C.P." specification in the tackle supply catalog means "no color preserver" needed.)

Thread sizes recommended for various rods:

- 00 for fly rods and ultralight freshwater rods

- A for light saltwater and most freshwater spin and casting rods

- D for medium to heavy freshwater rods

- or light-action saltwater spin and casting rods

- E for average saltwater surf and trolling rods

Note: Most rods will use size A. I use E for everything including bucktail jig-making. It's a little heavy for most rod guide uses, but it simplifies my inventory.

The drawings at right, courtesy of Gudebrod, illustrate how to wrap a new or replacement guide on a rod. Heavy-duty trolling or surf rods should get one layer of underwrap before installing the guide. For more detail on rod building, consult the publications and vendors listed in the Resources section.

Once the guide has been wrapped on the rod, apply the recommended color preserver to the thread and let it dry. Then, mix the two-part clear epoxy and apply it evenly to cover the thread. The epoxy will run before it sets up and form an ugly glob on the lowest point of the rod. *To avoid this, immediately after coating, slowly rotate the rod until the epoxy sets up.* I use epoxy with a 5-minute setup time for this reason. If the expert advice in a manufacturer's book doesn't agree with my system, follow its recommendation, and you can't go wrong. Manufacturers know their products. So far, clear 5-minute epoxy has worked for me.

A broken or chipped rod tip is easily replaced. To remove the old tip, carefully apply low heat to soften the heat-setting cement and remove the tip gently. If you use too much heat, the tip of the rod itself can be damaged. I have done this—the tip

Wrapping a New Rod Guide

1.

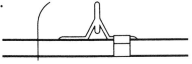

lay thread end over

2.

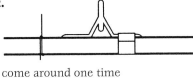

come around one time

3.

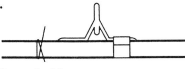

form a locking x

4.

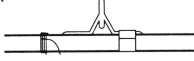

a few more turns

5.

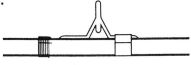

trim loose ends

6.

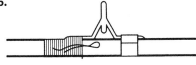

install pull through loop

7.

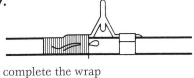

complete the wrap

8.

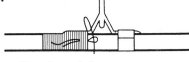

run line through loop

9.

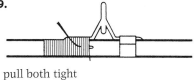

pull both tight

10.

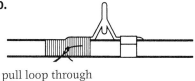

pull loop through

11.

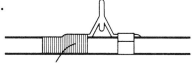

all the way through

12.

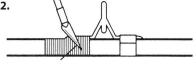

trim loose end

GUDEBROD

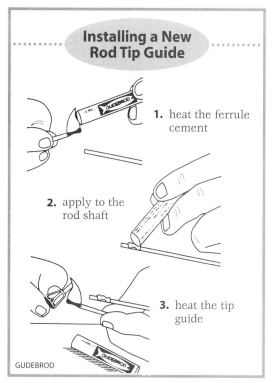

Installing a New Rod Tip Guide

1. heat the ferrule cement

2. apply to the rod shaft

3. heat the tip guide

GUDEBROD

became mushy and drooped over. There was no option but to cut off the soft part of the tip and use a larger diameter replacement tip, which did not noticeably change the rod's action.

To install a new tip, first heat the end of a stick of ferrule cement and apply it to the end of the rod. Before the cement sets up, slide the new tube-type tip on the rod and adjust it to align with the rod guides. When the cement hardens, carefully peel away the excess on the rod shaft. Epoxy can be substituted for ferrule cement if necessary.

Replacing rod guides and tip-tops can be so much fun that the reader might be tempted to build a custom rod from components. Many fancy touches like diamond

wraps and initials can be added by the home craftsperson. A complete set of matching rods can be built for the angler's boat in colors matching his or her tackle box, boat, trailer, and tow car. It has been done. You may decide to go into the rod business. Repairing that first rod can be addictive. Beware!

Inexpensive Rod Winding Lathe 114

Anglers who have only an occasional need to refurbish a favorite rod or replace a damaged guide can make a handy rod winding lathe from a pair of inexpensive Stanley

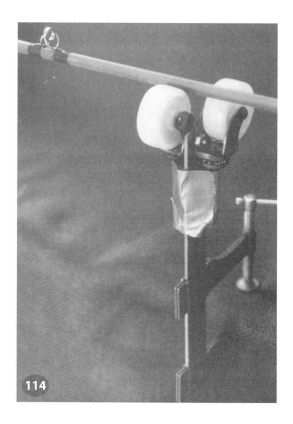

114

#H-157, 6-inch C-clamps and a set of four nylon casters.

My caster wheels were $1\frac{1}{2}$ inches in diameter with a swiveling shank, although any casters up to 3 or 4 inches in diameter can be used.

To assemble the two holders that make the rod winding lathe, first attach the C-clamp to the workbench top with the longer standard facing up. Then, hold the caster wheels in place, one on each side of the C-clamp standard, so you can mark the caster side plates and the standard for drilling. Make sure the outside radii of the casters overlap to provide a shallow V in which to rest the rod under repair.

Then, drill a small hole in each caster side plate and a matching hole in the C-clamp standard. A small nut and bolt will hold everything together. A piece of tape around the shank of the caster will keep the caster shafts aligned. Make two of these C-clamp rod holders—one to support each end of the rod being repaired.

In use, the rod holders are clamped to the edge of a workbench or table with the caster wheels facing upward and about 3 or 4 feet apart, depending on the length of the rod under repair. A rod placed in the V formed by the casters will be held in a comfortable working position and can easily be rotated by hand.

For infrequent repairs, rod winding thread can be tensioned by feeding it

The author with his rod winding setup on his living room coffee table.

through the pages of a telephone book, but serious rod rebuilders will want to use a thread-tension vise available from tackle suppliers.

A more elaborate rod winding lathe can be made by attaching the same nylon casters to blocks of wood that can be adjusted along a 5- or 6-foot piece of 1-by-6-inch shelving board, but then storage is a problem.

I have successfully used my simple rod winding lathe to rewrap rods of all sizes, from ultralight graphites all the way up to an antique 26-ounce bamboo big game rod tip.

You can quickly and inexpensively make the caster and C-clamp rod winding lathe. It stores easily, and the rod holders can still be used for their original purpose—as C-clamps.

Position a rotisserie motor shaft under and parallel to the rod. Connect the shaft and rod with rubber bands to rotate the rod slowly while the thread-covering epoxy sets up.

Repairing a Broken Rod   115

Breaking a favorite fishing rod can cause a lot of anguish. You and that old wand have been together through a lot of fishing, and you can't bear to toss it out.

Help is on the way with suggestions from one of my fishing buddies, Jack Stovall. He has repaired several of my favorite fish sticks—it looks so easy I might try it the next time I bust a rod.

First, save a few old fishing rods, or ask your friendly tackle shop owner to save a

few old rods for you instead of trashing them. Strip off the old guides and save them if they are in good condition. Sections can be cut from these old rods to make repair sleeves for the next rod you break, as shown below.

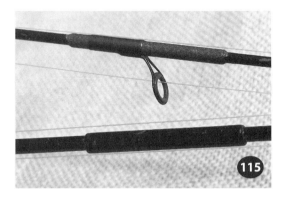

Stovall first measures the diameters up-rod and down-rod of the break. It helps if you use a micrometer for extreme accuracy, but it's not necessary. Rods are tapered somewhat, so you want to find a section from one of your junk rods that will fit above and below the break on your repairable one.

If the break is nearest the reel seat, the rod's inside diameter might be large enough to accommodate an internal splice. This is not likely because rods almost always break near the tip.

The most likely repair, in my personal experience, will require a sleeve on the outside of the rod. Once you have selected a section of the junk rod where the inside diameter of the sleeve equals the outside of the repair area, and have done a fit check, you're ready to epoxy. Mix the two-part epoxy (Stovall uses West System), and apply a thin coat on the inside of the sleeve and the outside of the repair area. Fit the pieces together with the rod guides aligned and wipe off any excess epoxy. Apply a very thin coat of epoxy on the outside of the repair.

To prevent a lopsided glop of epoxy from forming, rotate the rod slowly until the epoxy sets up. Slow-drying epoxies like West may need a long time to set, while a 5-minute epoxy could save you a lot of rod rotating.

If you used a yellow rod sleeve on a black rod, and don't want the repair to stand out like a bandaged thumb, paint the repair to match the rod *after* the epoxy is set up and hard. If the repair happened to be at the previous site of a rod guide, a new guide can be wrapped on over the sleeve.

I notice no difference in the action of my repaired rods, and they have taken their share of fish since the fixing without crunching or creaking.

Rod Tips

116 Ready-rigged fly rods often won't fit in standard boat rod holders. Upright plastic surface-mount rod holders can be modified to accept a fly rod with a reel attached by sawing a lengthwise slot in the rod holder slightly wider than the width of the fly reel's foot. Be sure to protect the delicate rod tip with foam plastic insulation from beating against a cabin or T-top in rough seas.

117 When transporting several rods that are ready-rigged to fish with a lure's single hook engaged in a rod guide, keep them from tangling together by wrapping the length of line between the tip-top and the lure once around the rod and securing it around a rod guide. Naturally, this system won't work if the rod's lure has treble hooks. It is hard to explain but easy once you try it. Once you get the hang of it, and use the system, your gear won't wrap itself together in a tight bundle that

takes time to unravel. Or, you could cover each rigged rod with a section of foam pipe insulation.

118 It is often recommended that older rod guides and tip-tops (and modern ceramic guides) be checked for grooves by pulling a piece of pantyhose through them to test for snags. This is an excellent idea, but guides and tip-tops can also be checked by close visual inspection as in the photograph below. This badly chipped rod tip escaped detection until it began to fray one of the new superlines.

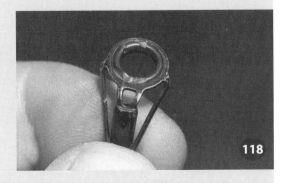

118

119 For those who don't like to hang lure hooks in a guide for fear of damaging the ceramic, loop a rubber band through the guide and attach the lure to that. Or, simply hang the lure's hook in the guide's bridge.

120 Keep a small bottle of clear fingernail polish in your tackle box in case rod windings become frayed while you're on a trip.

121 Rugged rod cases can be easily made from PVC pipe and fittings. Several rods can be packed in a case made from 4-inch-diameter, thin-wall septic drain-field pipe assuming they will be transported in the angler's vehicle. But, when traveling on airlines or other public transportation, make the rod case from stronger, thick-wall schedule 40 PVC pipe. After measuring the longest rod you plan to use, add an inch or two for packing (I use an old bedsheet intertwined around the rods), and cut the pipe to length. Using PVC cement, glue a solid pipe cap to one end of the pipe. I glued a threaded clean-out fitting with a screw-in plug to the opposite end

121

of the pipe. This plug can be made captive by drilling a small hole in it and another hole nearby in the rod case and attaching it with 100-pound-test mono leader. Make a carrying handle out of nylon rope or a rubber tie-down tied around the case at each end and securely taped in place.

122 Roller guides need constant attention. Trolling rod maintenance is often delegated to the first mate on a charter boat—roller guides are checked before each offshore trip. Rollers must roll, or else line can become abraded and weakened, and a possible record fish lost. Although modern aluminum oxide or silicon carbide ring guides have replaced roller guides on many trolling rods, roller guides are still popular for wire line, and roller tip-tops are still used on many light tackle and big game rods. Constant maintenance is the price of success. Disassemble the roller guides, clean off the caked salt with soap and water, then lubricate the roller surfaces.

123 One recent lightweight roller guide is designed for IGFA (International Game Fish Association) line tests from 2 to 20 pounds. Its single foot is mounted on the rod facing the butt. It is used mainly on casting and light-duty trolling rods. Light-tackle anglers find that roller guides cause less friction (longer casts) and less line abrasion on very light lines (less chance to lose a fish). Anglers who use wind-on leaders to get a fish closer to the boat might pay particular attention to their knots, since these small roller guides have a smaller aperture. A small dab of Teflon gel lubricates the guide's rollers.

124 If you lose a rod overboard and the water is too deep to see it, first toss a weighted buoy at the spot. Then open a fish stringer's snaps (or tie on a series of blunted treble hooks) and drag the array across the bottom on a fishing line.

125 If the rod ferrules are stuck, the way old-timers take a rod apart still works: grip the stubborn rod horizontally behind your knees with both hands and move your knees apart. This gives you a straight pull and more leverage. Try not to twist the rod. Metal ferrules should be cleaned and lubricated by wiping a bit of oil from the side of your nose on the male ferrule before reassembly.

126 Small light sticks or tiny bells on the tip of a surf rod make good bite detectors at night. Also, the space between two rod guides near the tip-top could also be covered with luminous tape or paint so you could see rod movement in the dark.

127 One rod maker designed a rod with several light-emitting diodes (LEDs) imbedded along the length of the blank. The batteries and a switch were in the handle. Midnight anglers would not only know just where and what their rod was doing,

but also they would be treated to a dazzling display of lights similar to the Fourth of July!

128 Two other rod makers were competing to get first dibs on a "variable action" rod. If an angler doesn't like a wimpy rod, the competing rod designers opined, he or she could adjust it to pool-cue stiffness in a heartbeat with a twist of the handle. One designer's solution was to put hydraulic fluid in the core of the rod so it could be "loaded" differently. The other maker was going to change the distance between a "rod within a rod." Think of the entertainment value on a dull fishing day if you had a combined "line-of-lights" and "variable stiffness" rod!

129 Jack Stovall (in photograph below, measuring his grandson Henner's spotted

129

sea trout) has a handy fish ruler right on his fishing rod. Stovall painted lines an inch apart on his favorite rod above the reel seat. It saves digging around in the tackle box for a ruler when in doubt—or if there is a cash pool on the longest fish.

130 To store long rods on a garage or basement ceiling, I used 6-inch-long screw hooks and bent the "hook" part wider to accommodate rod handles. The garage ceiling has wallboard on it, so it was easy to lay out the pattern of the rod hangers. I found the joists above the wallboard and drew light pencil lines 48 inches apart on the ceiling to indicate the joists above. These were far enough apart to support most rods, two hooks to a rod.

Then, I made tick marks 8 inches apart along each line for the screw hooks. This spacing works well for even the largest of

130

Fishing rods hung from screw hooks in the garage ceiling.

my reels. I punched small holes through the wallboard to start the hooks and twisted them in until they were firmly embedded in the joists. Luckily my ceiling height is just right for me to reach up and grab a reel to take the rods down.

131 To keep fishing rods from getting tangled, I made a floor-standing rod rack from PVC pipe and some leftover pieces of plastic central vacuum system pipe.

I use the rack when I give talks at shows and to fishing groups. It saves the embarrassment of trying to untangle rods and lines while an impatient audience twiddles its collective thumbs. The same materials could be adapted to just about any space or similar task on your boat or in your garage.

I started with a rectangle made from 1-inch ID schedule 40 PVC pipe as the base. Six Ts had an outside diameter that fit the inside diameter of six pieces of $1\frac{5}{8}$-inch ID gray plastic vacuum system pipe that hold the rods vertically. Four 90-degree ells made the corners.

Before assembly, the vacuum system pipe was flared on one end by heating it with a paint-peeling heat gun. When the plastic was soft, it was flared over the outside of a large tin funnel.

⚠ **Wrap a rag around the pipe and wear heavy gloves as you flare it.**

The pipe was glued together with PVC cement.

131

PVC floor-standing rod rack.

132 Shorter rods stored in my garage are hung by their eyes on cup hooks. I do not recommend this, and rod manufacturers won't either, but if you're careful, you won't damage the tip-tops.

Spacewise, I had no other option but to store them between the garage sink and the well water tank. An old wooden chair back in my junk bin, shaped like an arc, was hung on the wall like an inverted U, and cup hooks were spaced about 4 inches apart, screwed into the side facing away from the wall. It holds eight rods, rigged and ready for fishing.

132

Hanging rod rack made from old chair back.

Reels

Reel Drags 133

In 1898, Dr. Charles Fredrick Holder took a tuna weighing 183 pounds off Catalina Island. In the light of today's technologically superior tackle, that doesn't seem like a great feat. But, here's the hooker. His reel had a direct drive handle but no drag. When a fish of that size suddenly pulls on a reel of that vintage, the most immediate problem is to get your body parts out of the way of a backward-spinning buzz saw of a handle. The next immediate problem is avoiding a gargantuan backlash. Those minor perplexities taken care of, you have about one nanosecond to decide how many layers of thumb print you are willing to sacrifice to catch a fish. Remember, in those days the only pressure an angler could bring to bear on his tuna was by clamping his thumbs on the reel spool. Even if he had a heavy leather thumbstall, he must have had the soul of a Spartan to ignore the heat.

About the turn of the twentieth century, William Boschen, working in the cellar workshop of Thomas Conroy's New York tackle store, designed the multiple-disk drag and nonreversing handle that made possible sportfishing as we know it today. Boschen used a reel incorporating his new design in 1913 to catch the first rod and reel swordfish, effectively stifling those who had ridiculed him. He did not patent his magnificent invention. Not all of us have the

opportunity or desire to tangle with a swordfish, but every sport angler who has ever heard a reel drag sing owes a debt of gratitude to William Boschen.

Serious tournament anglers set their drags through the bend of the rod, in the fish-fighting position. The line is threaded through the guides and tied to a spring scale. A friend holds the scale and calls out the "pounds" drag setting as you back away holding the rod in the fighting position and adjust the drag. This procedure is best done outside. Line "pops" have given me some dandy dents in the living room ceiling to prove it.

Some big-game anglers recommend a striking drag of about one third of the line test and a fighting drag of about half of line test. Stiffer rods require a slightly lesser setting than limber ones. Lever drag reels of the Fin-Nor type give the angler the benefit of setting both striking drag and fighting drag and simply moving the lever to change settings.

Most of my reels are not lever drags, however, and I set them to a little less than half of line test and leave them set there for the season. If a fish manages to take out half the line on a reel, the reduced diameter of the line on the spool can double drag tension, and a large amount of line in the water also adds drag. In that case, I scientifically loosen the drag—and cross my fingers.

Rod guide types have a bearing on drag settings. Ring guides offer more friction than roller guides, but roller guides need more maintenance, as discussed in tip 122.

Those of us who have fished for more

The author's king mackerel is a result of good reel maintenance.

than three decades have noticed how much smoother reel drags are lately. While alternating leather and steel washers compressed on a spindle or axle were once the backbone of reel drag technology, other materials that are slicker and more heat-resistant are used now. Teflon, felt, stainless steel, aluminum, titanium, cork, and various composites in numerous combinations are finding their way into reel drags lately.

Another interesting development is the dual-drag reel (see photograph at right). The Shimano Bait Runner spinning reels incorporate two separate drag systems. One

drag is set lighter for hook-setting when a fish strikes the bait. When the angler reels the handle, the second, heavier drag comes into play for the fight.

Lever drag reels can also be set up for a dual-drag situation. By first placing the lever against its stop and setting the fighting drag at about one-third line strength, then backing the lever off to about half that for setting the hook as a running fish takes the bait, the angler can then place a mark with a permanent marker on each side of the lever's quadrant plate. That way, the angler has two reliable drag settings—one for hook-setting, another for fighting the fish.

Most of us have fished for years using the "feels-right" school of drag setting, in which you pull some line off the spool and adjust the drag until it "feels right." But if we intend to use William Boschen's wonderful invention to its fullest—say to try for the IGFA's 10-1 Club where the fish caught must weigh 10 times line test—we had better spend some time tweaking up our reel drags.

That time is now.

Reels set up for dual-drag action.

Line Reminder   134

How soon we forget! How long has that line been on that reel? And, what kind was it?

My solution is a piece of yellow waterproof plastic tape attached to the reel foot before putting the reel on the rod.

The date, line type, and pound test are marked with a Sharpie permanent marker with a fine-point tip.

I try to replace the line on my reels every year, more frequently if it has been in heavy use.

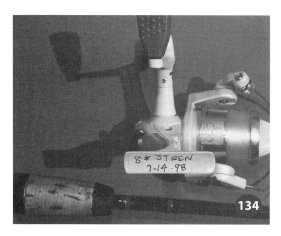

Write the date and line info on waterproof tape and place it on the reel foot.

Fishing Reel Maintenance   135

If you want your fishing reels to last and perform well, constant attention and maintenance will help. A visual inspection after every trip might be a pain, but it can pay off in the long run.

Make sure that line rollers on spinning reels really roll. If they don't roll, the line will cut a groove in the roller and weaken the line. Line should fill the spool within $1/8$ inch or so for best casting performance. Bail-return springs should be replaced if they don't close the bail smartly. Reel manufacturers recommend that drags be loosened between trips. Not many of us do that, but drags should be loosened in the off-season on all reels. If the rod tip bounces up and down as line is pulled off the reel, this means the drag is jerky and could break the line, so the drag washers need maintenance.

All reels should be cleaned and relubed at least once a year, preferably in the off-season. If you don't have an off-season, pick your own schedule and stick to it. Reels that get hard, everyday use should get more frequent maintenance. Most reels can be cleaned and relubed by the average angler. However, I would leave maintenance of off-shore lever drag reels to the manufacturer or a reliable tackle shop. These reels are far too complex for an average shade-tree mechanic like me to disassemble and maintain.

Here are the tools you'll need: screwdrivers (use screwdrivers with nontapered blades on high quality reels because a tapered blade can tear up a screw slot), assorted nut drivers or a $1/4$-inch-drive socket set, a small tin can with kerosene to clean off the old grease (no open flames nearby), an old toothbrush (not to be reused on teeth), plenty of old newspapers spread liberally around to absorb the mess, fresh new grease, and one or more paper egg cartons (paper cartons rather than the foam plastic cartons absorb the excess kerosene better) to hold parts sequentially as the reel is disassembled. It also helps to have the reel parts list and diagram handy in case your memory fails and you suddenly have questions about how all those parts relate to each other. You can also take a Polaroid photograph or use a camcorder to record the disassembly sequence.

I disassemble a reel with regular screwdrivers, but I make sure not to use undersized ones that chew up the screw slots. As each part is removed from the reel, I put it in the can of kerosene and scrub it with the toothbrush to remove dirt and old grease.

 Please do not use gasoline for cleaning reel parts—it is too dangerous! *I've had friends seriously burned when gasoline ignited from flames or a spark. Kerosene is also flammable, and care must be taken in using it, too.*

When cleaned, each part goes into a separate sequentially numbered depression in the egg carton. Drag washers are cleaned and restacked in the order they came off their axle or spindle for reassembly. Broken or badly worn parts should be replaced at this point.

On some of my old spinning reels, alternate drag washers were made of leather and

Setup for disassembling a fishing reel for cleaning and maintenance.

steel or brass. If the leather was badly compressed or worn, I cut a new washer out of an old leather wallet. On a 1950s Luxor spinning reel, I found that the complete drag range from "off" to "pop the line" was only about half a turn of the adjusting knob when I experimented with hard drag materials.

Before reassembling a reel, I regrease drag washers and gears and return them to the reel in the reverse order from the way in which I removed them. I have tried several different types of grease on drag washers. Never Seez high temperature grease seems to work well, but it needs to be replaced every year or it will thicken. Teflon lubricants work well for some anglers. The green waterproof Drydene grease I use on boat trailer bearings seems to work as well as any.

Outdoor writer Tom Goodspeed recommends using a dab of STP. You can never go wrong with the reel manufacturer's own brand of lubricant. Take your choice, but you'll soon realize a clean, dependable, well-lubricated reel makes for a more pleasurable fishing trip.

Once all your reels are in good shape, you can keep them that way with frequent inspections and a freshwater rinse after each trip. Then let them dry out if you store them in an enclosed place. My reels are stored on their rods and hung on the garage ceiling, so they are dry before mildew or corrosion can damage them.

Some anglers spray their reels with WD-40 or a similar product to protect them, but these include petroleum-based distillates that might damage fishing line.

Reel-Filler Spool Tension Clutch   136

Two small pieces of old floor carpet, one on either side of a reel filler spool, make a simple adjustable clutch so new line can be applied to reels under tension.

Cut two 4-inch squares of old carpet and punch a hole with an awl through the center of each piece. Carpeting with a short nap seems to work best, but shag and berber also work. Then, thread one piece of carpet onto a screwdriver or an awl with the backing side toward the awl handle, then thread on the line filler spool, and last the other piece of carpet with the nap side toward the spool.

Place the pointed end of the awl in a shop vise and adjust it so the friction on the spool puts slight tension on the line being wound onto the fishing reel, as shown below.

Next, thread the new line through the rod guides. Spinning reel bails should be open when the line is tied to the spool. Line on level-wind reels is threaded through the line-leveling guide and tied to the spool axle; then the knot is pulled tight.

After winding a small amount of line onto a spinning reel against light tension, stop and lower the rod tip a foot or so. If the slack line twists into a tight coil, turn the supply spool of line over, and wind more line on. Check again for line twist.

Line twist is the bane of all spinning reel anglers. Your first cast with twisted line will result in a gob of tangled line coming off the spool and wrapping around the rod guides. Properly installing line on the reel can solve that problem.

Reel Protectors 137

Reels, sunglasses, and other items carried on fishing boats are likely to get scratched if not protected. I save old (clean) socks for that purpose.

Women's "footies" (really short, fluffy socks) make nice reel covers. A regular sock will protect sunglasses or other items.

Fishing Reel Line Removal 138

The simplest way to remove old fishing line from a fishing reel is with a small handheld electric drill (see photograph on page 96).

First, I tighten a piece of scrap wood about the size of a pencil in the drill's chuck. Then, I secure the rod with the reel on it in a vise with a thick rag to protect the handle—or simply have someone hold the rod.

Next, the end of the line to be removed is tied to the stick. Revolving spool reels are

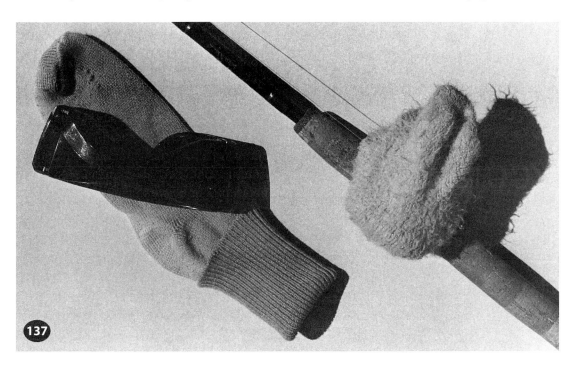

137

138

placed in "free spool." For spinning reels, remove line from the end of the spool. Run the drill until almost all the line is off the

spool, then go slowly to the end to prevent damage.

After cutting the old line at the reel spool, simply "unchuck" the piece of scrap wood and ball of old line and dispose of it. Some tackle shops have a recycling bin for old line.

Line is one of the least expensive items we use, and it is the weakest link between us and a possible record fish. Experts tell us it should be replaced frequently with new, fresh line.

This system can be used with all types and sizes of reels. It will save you time. The time you save is better spent fishing.

Reel Tips

139 Reversing the line on your reel can make the line last longer before you have to replace it. With the outside in, and vice versa, the unused inside portion will be practically like new. To get the line off the reel, I simply tie the outer end of the line to a tree and walk around the yard until all the line is off the reel. Then I cut the knot that attaches the line to the reel spool. As I walk, I slide the line through my fingers to detect nicks or wear. My route takes me around trees to get the longest path but not through any exposed dirt that the line could later transfer to the reel.

Next, I walk back to my starting point and untie the line from the tree and tie it to the reel spool. I wind the line back on the spool through my fingers again to

provide some tension and remove any dirt or debris.

140 One of the simplest ways to keep line on a spinning reel spool from unraveling is to tie a knot in a rubber band and slip it over the line on the spool. The knot becomes a "handle" to remove the rubber band.

141 Trolling rotating lures like spoons and in-line spinners often twists fishing line. To remove the twist, let the line out behind a moving boat with no terminal tackle attached—not even a snap swivel. Dragging the line through the water provides enough tension to untwist the line. Then reel in the line.

142 Some anglers claim they get longer casts with a spinning reel if they rub a bit of car wax on the lip of the reel spool.

143 Would you believe there is a simple fix for backlashes? Place your thumb (use two or three fingers for wider reels) on the spool and wind a couple of revolutions. Then, put the reel in "free spool" and pull the backlash out. I've tried it lots of times—it works most of the time.

144 Sometimes monofilament fishing line has been stored in tackle shops or your tackle box too long. If your line has a dull, powdery look, it's probably out of date and has started to decompose. It has reduced strength and will break easier in this condition. When the new "superlines" begin to fray, replace them or reverse them, too.

145 Insect repellent can play havoc with the finish on fly lines (as well as that of many other plastic articles), so rinse any bug juice off your hands thoroughly before handling fishing equipment.

146 Superlines are so "slippery" they will often slide around the spool if not properly anchored to it. If you keep tightening your drag and you are able to pull out line anyway, check to see if the spool is rotating. If the spool is not rotating, remove the superline (I walked mine off around the yard), and tie several yards of monofilament to the spool first. Then tie the other end of the mono to the end of your superline with a blood knot (see page137), then wind it on the reel. If you had the reel spool filled to the brim originally, you may have to cut a few yards off the end of the line to offset the mono you installed.

147 Superline often requires monofilament leaders to fool the fish. In a reverse situation, several Florida anglers use mono line on their reels and superline as a toothy-critter leader.

148 Fly anglers in search of record fish often need more backing on their new, large arbor reels. Some have replaced their Dacron backing with braided superline, which is much smaller in diameter per line test and allows more backing. The trick to installing a superline on any reel is to put it on under pressure, making sure to weave it back and forth as it goes on the reel. You want it to overlap in a crosswise fashion or it will bury in the underlying wraps and possibly break off a fish, bust a rod, or tear off a rod guide or two. Dacron stretches about 13 percent, braided superline stretches less than 4 percent, so fish might need to be played with a bit more finesse when using superline for backing.

149 Superlines are so thin for their strength, and so slippery, that anglers who try to pull on the line to dislodge a plug stuck in or around structure can cut themselves right to the bone! Bass anglers wrap the line several times around a 6-to-8-inch length of dowel for extra leverage and safety.

150 It is also possible to break your fishing rod since the superlines are not as forgiving as monofilament. Set the hook gently!

Lures

Lure Modifications 151

Innovative anglers often enjoy making or modifying their baits, always looking for the "ultimate lure" that will make the difference between a full stringer and a busted trip. Some modify lures for other reasons: the pure satisfaction of catching a fish on something you made; something to do in the winter; replacing dangerous treble hooks with single ones; or simply removing treble hooks to make it easier to release fish so you won't have so many to clean or give away.

Sharp readers will ask: "If single hooks are so great, why don't the manufacturers rig every lure that way?" Good question. The answer, according to a Pradco representative (makers of Heddon, Cotton Cordell, and Rebel, for example) is that single hook plugs don't sell. Tests of sales from side-by-side displays of treble hook plugs next to the same lures with single hooks were interesting: all the treble hook plugs sold out, but no single hook lures moved. Buyers equate the number of hooks with numbers of fish caught. But, don't feel guilty if you buck the multiple treble hook trend—single hook lures account for plenty of fish.

It's a lot of fun to modify or make your own lures. And it's a real thrill to see a fish bite on some crazy contraption that was born in your own fevered brain. There is no lure too silly to show to a fish. I know—I do it all the time.

Take Bill Cannon of Cambridge, Maryland—his well-decorated 1-ounce sassy shad lure is shown below. Bill wanted to cover all the bases in one superb lure for weakfish. In some areas like Delaware Bay, weakfish like purple worms. Bill added one. Stinger hooks often spell the difference between a hooked fish and a lost one. He added one with yellow feathers. A large whole shrimp topped off the conglomeration, which, in deference to his last name, I dubbed the "Cannon Ball." We caught weakfish up to 14 pounds on this lure combo, so don't make fun of it.

The Cannon Ball lure.

If necessity is the Mother of Invention, and imagination the Father, then it follows that innovation is the offspring. Let's take a look at some lures these parents bred in my home workshop.

In the photo below, ¹/₂-ounce Rat-L-Traps #1, #2, and #3 have been modified, with varying success. The top Trap #1 carries a single jig hook with the barb mashed down instead of two trebles. A jig hook was used so it would ride upright and not snag things, and a 4-inch swimmertail grub decorates the hook. The lure's nose digs down when retrieved, so the lure

rides at a 45-degree angle with the grub swimming behind. Does it catch fish? Well, during one striped bass season, this lure caught stripers on certain days. Other days, fish would slam it hard and not get hooked.

If you've ever cleaned a striper that had alewives stacked head-to-tail like sardines in its stomach, you'll know that fish sometimes hit lures head first, sometimes tail first. With two trebles, I might have hooked every fish, but with meager bag limits, who needs to catch every fish? Also, the single barbless hook made it easy to release un-

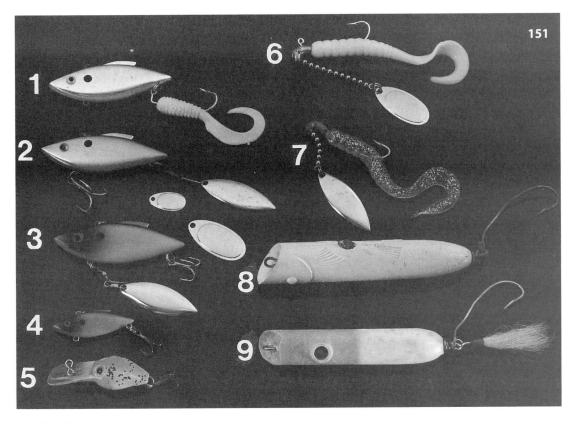

151

Modified lures #1 through #9.

dersized fish. Largemouth bass in my pond snagged this lure every cast, suggesting they didn't decide to grab it until it rattled through their living room, then they had to catch it from behind.

Rat-L-Traps #2 and #3 have spinner blades in place of their belly or tail treble hooks. Largemouth bass and stripers liked both of these combinations, with the belly treble rig catching better, but a single tail treble was more weed free. I used a #12 snap swivel to attach the blades, trying both French and willow spinner blades with equal success.

Lure #4 shown on the previous page is a ⅛-ounce Tiny-Trap, and lure #5 is a ⅕-ounce Storm Pee Wee Wart—both with their belly treble hooks removed. These tiny lures are deadly on white perch in the shallows in midsummer. The Wart wiggles a little deeper, but the perch will come up 2 feet to grab a Tiny-Trap. An active 11-inch white perch can sink a tiny treble in your finger in a heartbeat, so that's why I remove the belly treble. The scars are gone now, but the memory remains. I tried a single #4 jig hook instead of the tail treble but missed too many strikes.

For those who like to mold their own bucktail jigs, #6 and #7 are ⁵⁄₁₆-ounce Pony Head jigs cast in a Do-It mold. A 2/0 #635 jig hook was used. Instead of using a #12 barrel swivel for the spinner blade, I substituted a Netcraft #61 bead chain cut in two pieces of different lengths, one for each lure. A split ring at the end of the bead chain allows attachment of a French or willow leaf blade. They were decorated with a

6-inch white or chartreuse swimmertail worm. Some makers paint their jig heads, some don't. The fish don't seem to mind either way. A tow test in the bathtub will help the experimenter decide on bead chain length and blade preference. I liked seven beads and a willow leaf. Did it catch fish? No and yes. Pond bass ignored it, but Chesapeake Bay striped bass seemed very happy to see it.

Surface popping plugs #8 and #9 are just as productive as those with two treble hooks but make it easier to release fish, particularly if you file or mash down the hook barb. Remember, though, if you remove the belly treble hook on a surface popper, you have to substitute a small piece of ballast in the belly to make the plug ride upright. The white Herter's popper #8 (no longer available) has a small slug of lead in its belly hole. Lure #9 is a factory-made Z-faced Atom Popper that comes with a belly weight. A small piece of bucktail at the tail helps face this lure toward the angler for a better "pop."

There are lots of things to do with spinner and buzz blades. The saltwater-size spinnerbait #10 in the photograph opposite was cast in a modified Herter's "Popeye" jig mold. (Herter's once sold fishing lures.) Heavy wire (0.045 inch) was necessary for this Godzilla-strength spinnerbait. A French spinner blade and bucktail hair complete the rig. This is a great striper lure in summer or early fall before the first cold snap when the water clears. In clear water, stripers seem wire shy.

Baits #11 and #12 are similar to weighted

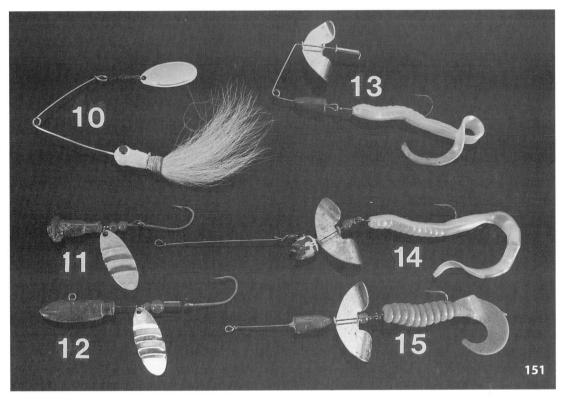

Modified lures #10 through #15.

walleye spinner lures. This is basically a good idea to combine sinker, spinner blade, and hook in one lure, but it is not popular everywhere. They were cast in old Herter's molds, using 0.045-inch wire in place of hooks. Then a clevis, spinner blade, and beads were added to the tail shaft before a loop to hold the hook was formed. Live or cut bait can be added to the hook, as can a 4-inch plastic grub in the color of your choice. Having the line attachment point on top of the weighted head is an advantage. The lure rides upright and keeps the spinner blade from twisting the line. These lures are better for casting. Trolling them would twist the line anyway. More about line twist later.

The top right buzzbait #13 in the photograph above slid nicely over lily pads in a bass river. We could see bass charging through the lily pads behind it, and when it reached open water, bingo! This one is easy to make with 0.035-inch wire, a buzzbait propeller, the grommet from a pop rivet, a bullet worm weight, and hook of your choice. Mine is decorated with a 7½-inch Culprit pearl worm.

The final two conglomerations in the photograph above are interesting: one is a great fish-getter, the other twists line before it hits the water. Lure #14 was molded with 0.035-inch wire in place of the hook in a ½-ounce ruby lips jig mold. Then a buzzbait propeller was added with a bead behind it. A long shank hook accommodates a 7½-inch Culprit worm. Unfortunately on the first cast, everything wrapped around the main line. A short piece of stiff wire leader solved that problem. This lure makes so much commotion and looks so silly underwater that when I caught stripers on it, I was probably more surprised than the fish.

Lure #15—while easily made from 0.035-inch wire, a bullet weight, a buzzbait propeller, a bead, and a hook—was a flop. It twisted line badly because the attachment point is in a direct line with the propeller shaft. I included this flopperoo as a bad example to show the reader that every modification isn't successful.

But, I'll keep trying until I make the "ultimate lure."

If one of your "ultimate lures" looks so good in the water you want to jump right in after it, stop right there. You've got a winner!

Make Your Own Plugs   152

"Holy cow!" Jack Stovall hollered, "Did you see that strike?" A big striper had grabbed Stovall's homemade copy of a famous bottleneck popper and wrapped it around a tree stump quicker than it takes to tell about it. Either the tree or the fish now owned the lure. I groaned. Stovall's beautiful, lathe-turned, airbrush-painted plugs are works of art. The one he gave me is in a trophy case, untouched. It's too pretty to fish.

Stovall tied on another handcrafted masterpiece. "I've gotta see that again," he said. It was a slow-motion replay of the same act. One pop next to the fallen tree and ka-plooey! The plug disappeared in the midst of a huge splash and a swirl the size of a bathtub. Our craftsman-angler sighed and tied on another shiny new plug. Next, a third replay, but in fast-forward. Somebody down there now owned three magnificently painted wooden works of art.

I saw Stovall rooting around in his tackle box.

"What are you looking for?" I asked.

"Something cheaper," he replied.

Three minutes, three lures lost—plugs that probably took at least 3 hours each to make. Was it worth it? You bet. The memory of those strikes will long outlast the pain of lure loss. And you can bet Stovall will be spending time the next long, cold winter making more lures to toss at that same log next May.

Some angler-craftsmen, like Stovall, can look at a lure, or even a picture in a tackle catalog, then go back to their shop and make a copy. And have a lot of fun doing it, too. They might make some changes in body style, paint the bait differently, or not paint it at all in the case of jigheads or spinner baits.

Stovall started making lures because he couldn't find modern wood versions of his favorites: Heddon's Lucky 13 and Vamp-Spook. Those and other oldies like the Creek Chub Darter were too valuable as "antiques" to toss at fish. Once, he made a Boone Castana look-alike because an origi-

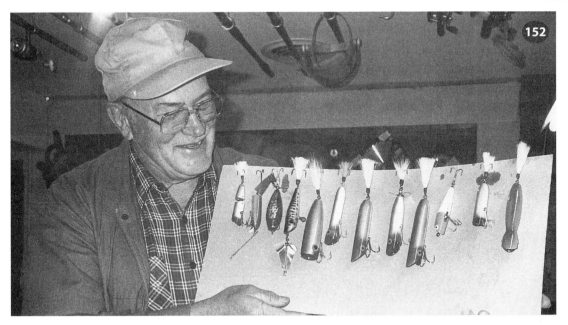

Jack Stovall with a display of his homemade plugs.

nal couldn't be found in the catalogs. Someone who had a Castana said it was a hot snook and speckled trout bait in Florida, where Stovall was headed on vacation. Was his version a great lure? You bet.

Although a wood lathe allows more flexibility in the design, good lures can be made from broom, shovel, or rake handles. Closet rod is another quick way to get a round piece of wood. A simple popper can be made by scooping out a concave nose and rounding off the tail.

"I like seasoned white cedar for its lightness," Stovall said. "Sometimes, dowel woods are too heavy—they won't float. Closet rod is OK if it's light enough." Stovall has a small wood lathe, so making lathe-turned lures is not a problem. He uses a Dremel tool to hollow out a concave face

for poppers. After shaping the body, he sands it on the lathe. Before painting, the plug gets three coats of auto paint primer. Some lures get a Rust-Oleum primer, with sanding between coats.

He always checks out his floaters in a tub of water before painting. For small fish lures, he uses small screw eyes for hook hangers. Larger lures, including those for big stripers, get brass sinker eyes for hook hangers, epoxied into drilled holes in the plug. He doesn't like split rings, so he makes open-eye hooks by cutting the eye of a treble with heavy duty diagonal pliers.

⚠ **If you try this, make sure you are wearing eye protection to avoid bits of metal flying off the hooks! Stovall attaches the hooks after the painting is finished.**

Hooks can be held in place with screw eyes unless big stripers and blues are expected. Drilling through the length of the plug so it can be through-wired gives the big-fish angler a feeling of security. The popper's tail hook can be decorated with bucktail hair to act as a rudder that keeps the lure aimed at the angler's rod tip after each "pop."

Painting lures has become an art form to Stovall. He paints his lures with an airbrush! Then he adds stick-on eyes, and the lure gets a last coat of clear varnish. His lures have already been weighted for proper balance. Stovall's baits have a dark topside and silver sides, and the bottoms are painted orange, yellow, or white. The cup on a popper's face is usually red.

Painting the lure gives the craftsperson a sense of pride, but fish are looking up at the bait's bottom. They see the plug in silhouette, and must quickly decide if it looks like lunch.

For the average angler just starting out to make his or her own plugs, it might be smart to buy some unpainted wood or plastic plug bodies from Netcraft, Cabela's, or other tackle suppliers. Finish them by painting and hanging hooks. Then decide whether to pursue the hobby of making them from scratch.

For those who want to go a step further, I suggest getting a copy of C. Boyd Pfeiffer's book *Modern Tackle Craft*, which goes into much more detail than can be included here (see the bibliography in the Resources section).

However, if you decide to make wood

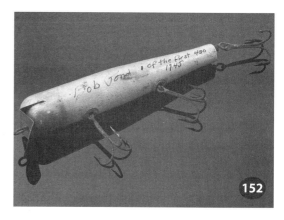

One of the first four hundred of Bob Pond's original handcarved Atom Plugs.

plugs from scratch, a band saw or jigsaw is necessary to cut out the blanks, and some shop tools like a saw, wood rasp, sander, and drill should be at hand.

Larger saltwater plugs are through-wired for strength, so a long electrician's drill bit is necessary.

Painting can be as elaborate as Stovall's airbrush decorating or as simple as two coats of enamel with a small brush.

You never know when you'll come up with a hot lure design, so it pays to experiment. It's not only fun during the winter doldrums, but the right lure could provide you with extra income.

Fifty years ago, Cape Cod striper angler Bob Pond turned out four hundred wooden swimming plugs, essentially superlarge Creek Chub swimmer look-alikes. Stripers loved them. Geyserlike eruptions under Pond's plugs reminded World War II–era anglers of the atom bomb explosions then in the news, so he called his lure the "Atom Plug." That lure, shown above, and others he designed provided Bob with a living for fifty years—plus some of the best fishing imaginable.

We should all be so lucky!

Making Bulletproof Bucktails 153

Bucktail jig-making is another way to cure the winter blahs. No one ever has enough of these effective lures. You will need a source of lead or lead substitute and a well-ventilated place to melt the metal, plus a jig mold, hooks, scissors, heavy leather gloves or oven mitts, thread and a bobbin, and a natural white or color-dyed bucktail.

⚠️ **Pouring lead into molds to make sinkers and jigs is dangerous. Always wear heavy leather gloves and use thick kitchen potholders when handling hot lead molds. Always work in a well-ventilated area when melting lead—it is toxic. Occasionally I melt old tire weights for sinkers (though softer lead is recommended), and pieces of rubber tire sometimes adhere to the weight. The smell of burning rubber in a lead pot will quickly remind you to open all windows and doors, if you haven't already! Always be careful when pouring into molds. A pocketful of hot lead is nothing to sneeze at!**

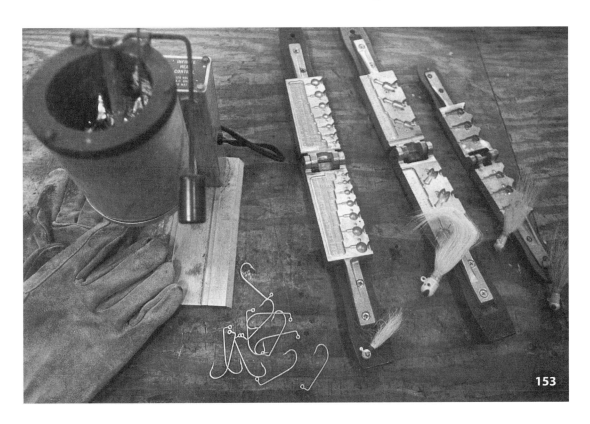

153

The personal dangers of working with lead have been known for decades. The environmental consequences are, in the opinion of this author, under debate.

Follow the mold maker's directions to make the jigheads, then let them cool. Years ago, I painted the heads with leftover white or yellow rustproofing enamel. It chipped badly. One good smack against a concrete bridge piling, and the paint was gone. Next I tried vinyl paints; the jigs were pretty and durable, but the paint fumes were unpleasant.

Lately, I've used powder paint with great success. Properly cured, this heat-setting epoxy powder is nearly bulletproof. I have dented the lead under properly prepared powder paint, but the lure's finish didn't even chip!

First, hold the jig by the hook with a pair of pliers. Then, heat the jighead with a heat gun until the lead or lead substitute is very warm to the touch. After stirring the powder paint to loosen it, dip the heated jighead into the powder, quickly remove it, and tap the hook on the container to dislodge excess powder. You can watch the paint turn to a nice glossy finish. If the finish is dull, heat it until it glosses. If the finish bubbled, the metal was too hot. Toss it away, or at bluefish.

Hang your painted jig to cool. One coat of powder paint is durable enough for average use. But, if you go one extra step, the finish is almost chip-proof. Hang the jig in the oven and bake it for 15 minutes at 300°F, then let it cool again.

Ron Adamecz of Annapolis, Maryland,

hangs six or eight bucktail jigheads on the rack of a toaster oven and heats them at 325°F, his ideal temperature for the black powder paint he favors. He modified the rack in his toaster oven with four bolts to accommodate the jigs. After removing the jigheads individually with a pair of pliers and dipping them in the powder paint, he hangs them to cool. When they are completely cool, he bakes them again in the toaster oven at 300°F for 10 minutes, then turns off the heat and lets them cool in the oven with the oven door open.

After the lead or lead substitute is cool, tie on the bucktail hair, lock the thread in place with a dab of superglue, and go fishing. For additional durability, I usually skip the superglue and slip a ³/₄-inch-long piece of ¹/₂-inch-diameter electrician's heat-shrink tubing over the jighead to cover the thread. Then I cover the bucktail hair with a piece of aluminum foil to prevent singeing and use the heat gun to shrink the tubing and lock the threads in place. One commercial jig maker wraps chemical-shrink tape over the thread. The resulting bucktail jig not only looks nice but also will outlast the average jig many times.

I have caught (and released) over two hundred stripers on one of my bulletproof bucktails, and it still has all its hair and paint, though the shrink tubing has been roughened by many striper gums. One of my jigs has been in use for three striper seasons!

Once the midwinter lure craftsperson gets in the swing of it with jig molds, hooks, wire, beads, and other goodies, experimenting with other lures like spinnerbaits comes

153

This shows the progression: heat-shrink tubing, tied bucktail, bucktail with tubing slipped over the thread, bucktail with tubing heated and shrunk.

naturally. Molding a 1-ounce jighead on a 0.047-inch wire spinnerbait form was a successful experiment for me. Basically a heavy-duty bass-style spinnerbait with bucktail hair dressing the head, my lure cast nicely on heavy spinning gear and caught a lot of shallow-water stripers.

Bass anglers can buy a spinnerbait mold and preformed wires to cut their labor. Spinnerbait heads and blades can be decorated with the previously mentioned powder paint; some lure makers even use an ear syringe to blow a contrasting shade of

powder paint on the background color before it cools. Very artistic!

⚠ **Don't use the ear syringe in your ear after it has held powder paint!**

Other accessories include all kinds of brass-and-glass noisemakers or clackers, high quality ball bearing swivels, and metal blades. Many of these designs are attractive to bass, but anglers must please themselves first before showing their creations to lower forms of marine life.

In-Line Sinkers as Lures 154

In-line sinkers with an eye at each end are designed to get a lure deeper by inserting them into a leader or the main fishing line. They are mostly used in trolling.

With the increased use of (expensive) deep-jigging lures that resemble a table knife handle, ingenious anglers began to make their own deep-jigging lures. One quick and inexpensive adaptation is to paint an in-line sinker and add a hook to one end of it with a split ring.

Two in-line sinkers are on the left in the photograph below, and two lures made from similar sinkers are on the right. The top lure was simply painted, and a hook was at-

154

tached. A stick-on eye was placed near the line tie eye. The bottom lure was also made from an in-line sinker, but it was pounded into a flattened shape with a hammer before it was painted and the hook attached.

In use, one tine is cut off the treble hook with a pair of compound wire cutters.

 However, use extreme caution if you do this: aim the tine to be severed away from yourself—it comes off at high speed and can imbed itself in an eye or other valuable body part! A double hook is much easier to remove from a fish's mouth than a treble, hence this extra step.

Jig Pouring Tips

155 When pouring jigs and sinkers, make sure you have good ventilation. Use heavy gloves and wear eye protection.

156 Use soft lead or lead substitute for jigs. Melted wheel weights often don't fill out the cavity of a jig mold very well but can be used for sinkers.

157 Good molds are worth their price. Cheap molds leave a lot of flash that has to be trimmed off. They also make lumpy jigs, which will give your friends a good laugh.

158 "Smoke" the mold with a candle flame before using. Carbon helps release jigs from the mold easier.

159 Heat the mold before adding hooks by pouring several jigheads without hooks. Save the resulting ingots for remelting.

160 Hooks must fit the mold neatly for best results. Overlarge hooks can keep the mold from closing all the way.

161 Some people give the jigheads one coat of paint before tying on bucktail hair.

When the hair is tied on, another coat of paint seals the thread. This does not apply to powder paint.

162 Custom-machined precision molds like the one made years ago for Bob Meushaw's famous Chesapeake Bay feather jigs might fit together so tightly air can't escape. That doesn't allow the lead or lead substitute to fill out the mold. Bob's machinist scribed several shallow lines across the mold's open faces to let trapped air out. (See photo below.)

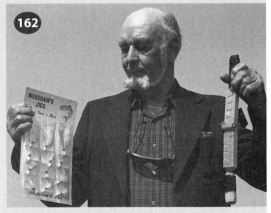

Bob Meushaw with his famous feather jigs.

163 Fine wire jig hooks give better penetration and bend easily when caught in a log or sometimes in a fish. Tinned jig hooks with an O'Shaughnessy bend (see photo at right) are better suited to saltwater applications and big fish.

164 Jig molds can be modified. Chuck Prahl's modified spinnerbait mold, shown at right, makes a great spearpoint bucktail jig that has become a very popular striped bass lure. Chuck used a Dremel tool with a round stone to make the concave recess in the mold for the #635T jig hook he wanted to use. The small channel where the spinnerbait wire exited the lure's nose was left alone—it leaves a

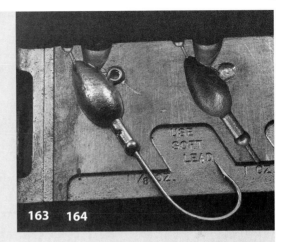

Closeup of Chuck Prahl's modified spinnerbait mold, which accommodates an O'Shaughnessy bend jig hook.

small amount of flash that can easily be trimmed.

Saltwater-Sized Thread Bobbins   165

Saltwater anglers who tie their own bucktail jigs can easily make a heavy-duty thread bobbin from lamp parts to accommodate heavy E size thread on 100-yard or larger spools. The bobbin can be customized to individual lure maker's needs.

To make my two bobbins (see bottom photo on page 110), I used the following parts:

- one piece of ⅜-inch all-thread lamp pipe in the proper length

- two ⅜-inch lamp pipe nuts

- one ⅜-inch pull chain switch bushing

- one piece of perforated car radio support strap ¾ inch wide by ¹⁄₁₆ inch thick by 6 inches long (from an old car radio installation)

- one ¼-20 bolt 2½ inches long

- one ¼-20 locknut

First, bend the radio support strap in a vise into a U shape to accommodate your spool of thread. Then, drill a ¹³⁄₃₂- or ⁷⁄₁₆-inch hole in the center of the U to fit the ⅜-inch lamp pipe.

⚠ **Tighten the strap in a vise while drilling.**

I used a 2-inch piece of lamp pipe on one bobbin and a 3-inch piece on the other one to allow enough clearance to wrap thread onto bucktail jigs with small or large heads.

First, remove any sharp edges on the lamp pipe or bushing that will cut or abrade your thread. Secure the lamp pipe to the U-shaped strap with two ³/₈-inch lamp nuts. Screw the ³/₈-inch pull chain switch bushing on the other end of the lamp pipe. Place the 100-yard spool of thread in the U and secure it with the ¹/₄-inch bolt and nut. Adjust spool tension by tightening the locknut.

A 14-inch piece of stiff leader wire bent double, as shown below, makes a good bobbin threader. Lamp parts are available from lamp or hardware stores. Radio support straps are available from car radio installers.

An "emergency" thread bobbin for tying hair on bucktail jigheads can be made from a short length of ¹/₈-inch or so diameter aluminum or copper ground wire, as shown at

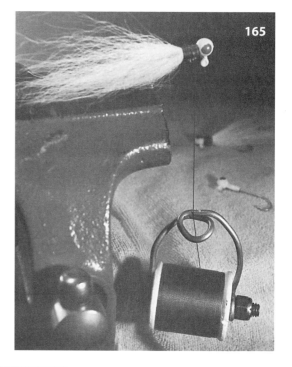

165

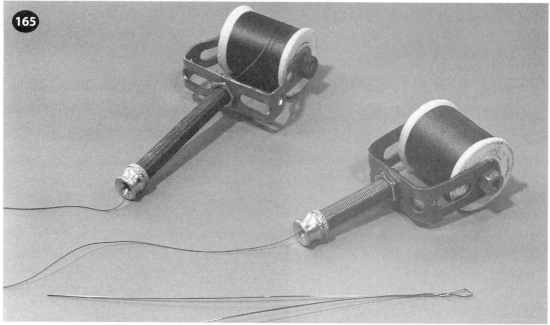

165

Heavy-duty thread bobbins for tying saltwater jigs can be made from lamp parts.

left. Make a circle bend on each end of the wire to accommodate the ¼-inch bolt and Nylok nut. Then bend a larger circle at the midpoint in the wire to make the thread captive. Tighten the nut so the thread bobbin does not drop.

In use, thread is pulled off the bobbin for a foot or so at a time, and the thread is wound onto the jighead by directing it through your fingers.

Rubber Cement for Bucktail Tying   166

Controlling a loose hank of bucktail hair while making those first few thread wraps to hold it in place on a jighead can be really frustrating for novice and even some expert tiers.

Atom Lure manufacturer Bob Pond passed on a tip that has been a big help to uncoordinated home tiers like me.

First, drop a glob of rubber cement onto a plastic lid. Cut a hank of hair off the deer tail and swish the cut end around in the rubber cement. Place several cemented hanks around the lid to dry as shown below. Then, with a jighead in the vise, scissor off squarely the cemented end of a clump of hair. Spread the hair evenly around the jig and secure it with thread. You'll find it stays in place and there are no loose hairs to fall out. Finish-wrap and superglue the thread, or cover it with heat-shrink tubing.

166

You can even work in a breezy area with rubber-cemented bucktail hair. It won't blow around like loose hair. A dab of rubber cement can eliminate the frustration factor and speed up bucktail jig tying for novice and pro alike.

Making Mini-Spinnerbaits   167

White perch and white bass are favorites on the table. They are both close cousins of the striped bass and are worthy opponents on ultralight spinning gear and mini-spinnerbaits. You can get a store-bought version for a dollar or so, but once you get the jig mold, lead or lead substitute, hooks, wire, round-nose pliers, ball-bearing swivels, and spinner blades, you can make hundreds of these perch-getters for nearly the same unit cost.

White perch love the author's homemade spinner-and-grub lures.

The difference is in the fun of making your own successful lures.

To make mini-spinnerbaits, I first cast about a hundred $\frac{1}{8}$-ounce and $\frac{1}{16}$-ounce jig-heads on #4 and #6 jig hooks. Paint them if it makes you happy, but perch and whites don't care. Next, buy or bend up some wire forms from 0.024- to 0.027-inch wire, copying a store-bought model. A pair of small electronics-sized round-nose pliers will make this job easier.

Then, attach a tiny jig to one end of the V-shaped wire form and a #12 snap swivel to the opposite arm of the wire. Add a #1 chrome French spinner blade (my favorite) or a #3 chrome Swiss Swing blade to the snap swivel. Next, add a 2-inch white (or your favorite color) plastic grub to the jig hook, and you're ready to fish.

A 'Poxy on Your Fly   168

Coastal fishing guides and tackle shops have noticed an ever-expanding interest in saltwater fly-fishing in recent years. Modern saltwater fly tackle and synthetic fly-tying materials have allowed briny anglers to go after bigger, toothier gamefish than flimsier freshwater fly gear would tolerate. Durable synthetics like crimped nylon have replaced polar bear and bucktail hair in many saltwater fly patterns. In addition, flies made of 5-minute epoxy are nearly indestructible, no matter how sharp a critter's dentures. Called Mother of Epoxy or MOE, these early flies have spawned the ever-increasing variety of artsy and colorful flies one sees now.

Bob Popovics of Seaside Park, New Jersey, is one of the mid-Atlantic area's best known MOE fly innovators. In 1974, his first MOE flies were "crude," he said, and made of polar bear and bucktail hair. Bluefish rapidly destroyed them. He tied some MOEs with Ultra Hair, and hair loss decreased. Surf and bay anglers soon found Popovics's epoxy-bodied flies were so tough you couldn't wear them out.

Both epoxy and silicone adhere well to fly-tying materials. Good. Both products also stick to hands, clothes, and tools with a terrible tenacity. Bad.

Lefty Kreh wets his hands in a cup of water containing six to eight drops of dishwasher Jet-Dry to keep them from sticking while shaping both 5-minute epoxy and silicone flies. Lefty now uses clear silicone caulk for fly bodies. "It's flexible, clear, and you can mold it with your fingertips as it starts to dry," Kreh says. "Silicone lets the feathers or hair work better than a hard epoxy body does. Also, fish might be more likely to hang on to a body of soft silicone. Sink rates are about the same for both epoxy and silicone-bodied flies."

MOEs can be balanced with soft wire, lead-free BB shot, or artificial eyes placed opposite the hook point to make the fly ride hook up. Doll eyes opposite the point of the hook make the fly ride hook down. Stiff mono can be tied in before epoxying as a weed guard.

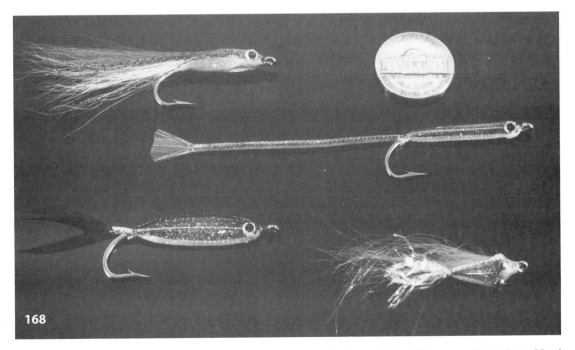

Clockwise from top left: Epoxy Silverside, Mylar Sand Eel, Stealth Fly, and Glass Minnow—all by D. L. Goddard of Easton, Maryland.

Beach or boat, epoxy-head streamer or MOE fly—any way you do it, be advised that saltwater fly-fishing is coming on fast.

Build some MOE flies and dunk them in the salt when big stripers or blues are around. You're in for a thrill.

Drapery Hooks Aid Anglers 169

Anglers have found many uses for the common drapery hook. For our purposes, the longer versions of the drapery hook are most useful. The short ones won't be long enough for some uses.

This versatile tool is inexpensive and has a sharp point and a "handle." It can be used to remove paint from lure eyes, help embed rattles in plastic worms, and clean out the ragged edges in holes through egg and bullet sinkers. Among other uses is the ability to pick backlashes out of level wind reels.

Some anglers carry one of these "tools" in their tackle box and replace it when it gets rusty.

The drapery hook in the center has many uses in fishing.

Lure Tips

170 Many lure and rig-making accessories—doll eyes, beads, yarn, glitter, and other goodies—can be found in craft stores. Let your imagination run wild.

171 Hit flea markets and garage sales for trinkets to add to, or make, lures. Old earrings can be added to spinnerbaits for extra pizzazz.

172 Other homey items for lure making include kitchenware. Some anglers haunt flea markets and garage sales looking for knives and spoons to make casting lures, the fancier the better for extra glitter. I made a deep-jigging spoon from an old stainless steel table knife, but it was impossibly hard to cut with a saw. I had to grind the blade off. Drilling a hole in each end of the handle for a large split ring allows for a hook at one end and the fishing line at the other. The bowl of a tablespoon makes a good wobbler, again by drilling two holes and adding a hook. Save the spoon handle to make yet another lure. Bend the handles for more action. Slap on a little paint, large eyes, or both. Try out their action in the bathtub or a local pond and make adjustments if necessary. These make great deep-jigging spoons in freshwater or salt water.

173 Add glitter and neon-enhanced fabric paints to all manner of lures including crankbaits, poppers, and plastics to attract fish.

174 Red and black waterproof Sharpie pens can be used to enhance the appearance of bucktail jigs. Use the black Sharpie to make stripes across the bucktail hair in a raccoon-tail pattern and the red marker to make a red "gill" on the head. Some anglers believe these enhancements help them catch more fish.

175 Carry a bottle or two of quick-drying nail polish in the boat. You may want to change the color of a lure on short notice. Anglers who use small jigheads coated with powder paint carry 35 mm plastic film cans of the material in different colors on their boats for the same reason. They warm the jighead with a cigarette lighter, dip it in the powder, and make a cast.

176 The eyes have it. Gamefish chasing baitfish are said to key on the eyes (see top photo, page 116). Add eyes, the larger the better, to jigheads, plugs, worm weights, and offshore trolling lures. Dab a common nail (with a head) in bright color paint to place the outer ring of an eye on your jighead, worm weight, or plug. After drying, dab a finishing nail (with no head) in black paint and make the center, or iris, of the eye. Colored glue from the craft store can be used to make eyes. Get two different, contrasting colors and apply them to worms, tube baits, and weights. Boyd Pfeiffer glues a single doll eye on the underside of his fly rod poppers—"that's what the

176

Eyes seem to attract gamefish.

fish sees," he says. Painted eyes, doll eyes, and stick-ons, covered with clear epoxy or varnish, could increase your catch ratio, some experts say.

177 Add a Rubbercor or pinch-on sinker to the lower leg of a spinnerbait to make it run deeper.

178 To add a rattle to a spinnerbait, slip a piece of heat-shrink tubing over the hook and put a rattle in it before shrinking the tubing with heat. A small rattle can also be superglued to a large spinner blade or placed inside a plastic grub before putting it on the hook.

179 Drilling holes in the outer tips of buzzbait blades will disturb more water as you pull the bait along. Some anglers drill holes in spoons for the same reason.

⚠ *Warning:* **always anchor a blade or spoon in a vise before drilling, because the drill bit can bind and spin the metal piece around like a knife blade.**

180 Tiny orthodontist's rubber bands (shown below) or snips of small-diameter tubing can be used on "R-shaped" spinnerbait or buzzbait wires in case the angler uses snaps or snap swivels. This keeps the snap from migrating up one or the other wires and tangling the line.

181 To use an old spinnerbait as a sinker, cut off the hook just behind the jighead, remove the spinner blades, and attach a

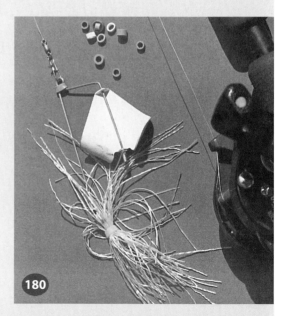

180

Tiny orthodontist's rubber bands can be used on spinnerbaits or buzzbait lures.

baited hook or short leader and lure instead. Attach the fishing line in the same place as you would normally.

182 Cut the jighead off an old buzzbait and bend a circle at the wire's end. Attach it to a floating Rat-L-Trap or other shallow-running crankbait. Buzz it along in the shallows.

183 Use a wooden coffee stirrer to make a slot, or use a drinking straw to hollow out a tunnel, in a plastic worm for a rattle or attractant. Fix the rattle in place with a dab of superglue.

184 Save your old bloodworms, says Ted Sheridan of Mr. Wiffle soft plastic lures. He squeezes out the "blood" and soaks his Mr. Wiffles in it. He takes spot, croaker, flounder, and sea bass with them. "I used one soaked bait all day," he says.

185 Plastic worms can be repaired with a match or a hot needle by heating the broken ends and holding them together until they bond.

186 Plastic bass worms can be fished efficiently by hooking them on a small ball jighead. If you want them to "float" higher in the water column on the retrieve in shallow water, use a flat (parallel to the bottom) jighead instead.

187 Zippered plastic bags are great places to store plastic worms and grubs. Because they can bleed together, store each color separately. I squish out the air and store

the rolled bags in a clear Plano #3700 box.

188 Jigheads can be rigged weedless in plastic tube baits. Simply hide the hook inside the tube.

189 Screw a French blade to the bottom of a jighead like a crankbait lip to make it "swim."

190 Another way to make jigheads, worms, or grubs weedless is to make some small coils from leader wire (looks like a coil spring) and make a loop in one end of the coil. The loop hooks into the jig's eye (center lure in the photograph below), and the grub or worm is threaded on the coil. Hide the hook point in the grub (far left).

191 Use bread bag wire ties to keep the worm or grub from sliding down the

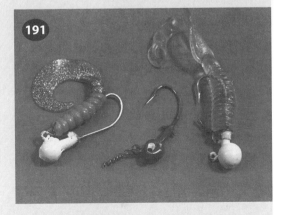

Left to right: *Ball-head jig with head of grub on coil of wire; jighead showing application of wire coil; and bread bag wire ties keep worm or grub in place.*

hook (far right lure in photograph on page 117)—or put a small dab of superglue gel on the hook shank before installing the plastic grub or worm.

192 Stuff a rigged tube-jig with cotton, using a toothpick, says outdoor writer Bob Jones, and soak the cotton with your favorite oil-base fish attractant. Works in freshwater or salt water, he says. I found a piece of sponge works, too. The stuffed tube will often float if rigged without a jighead.

193 Tube lure "tentacles" can be made to flare out better by gluing a small, round piece of sponge to the hook inside the tube—soak it with attractant if you like.

194 A soft tube or squid jig can be made almost weedless by threading a leader through the tube, sliding an egg sinker up the leader until it is inside the tube, then hiding the hook in the soft plastic.

195 Some anglers put pieces of rock salt into a tube bait to attract bass bites.

196 In similar fashion, says Capt. George Fromm of Neavitt, Maryland, a piece of rubber or plastic tubing glued to the shank of a bucktail jig's hook flares the hair out to make a more attractive bait. It can also hold a piece of pork rind farther up the hook shank.

197 According to Storm Lures, two baits are better than one, as evidenced by their "Double Bug," one Chug Bug behind another. Removing the tail hook on the front lure and coupling the two tail-to-head with a split ring can connect almost any two lures.

198 In addition to the lure modifications discussed previously, some lures work just as well if fished backward! Simply remove the tail hook and attach the line in its place. Then, split-ring the tail hook at the "front" of the plug. Bob Pond of Atom Lures saw Cape Cod anglers doing that to his big swimming plugs. His Reverse Atom plug was a big hit in 1947 and is still selling!

199 If you replace the treble hooks on a favorite plug with single hooks, be aware that the new hooks can change the balance of the lure. In some cases, you can clip off one tine of the treble to make a double hook without changing the plug's balance.

⚠ **Caution! Aim the pliers away from you; the clipped-off tine comes off like a bullet.**

If a large single hook replaces a treble, use a heavier split ring to keep the plug on even keel.

200 Weighting the tail of a popping or cigar-shaped surface plug makes it act like a dying baitfish when you stop its forward motion. It should lie face up, tail down, in the water. A small hole drilled in the popper's bottom near the tail will accommodate a piece of superglued lead-free solder. Several manufactured cigar-shaped topwater baits are weighted with a large steel bearing in a cavity near the lure's tail.

201 All manner of throwaway items can become fishing lures. Fountain pen bodies are made into poppers for striped bass and bluefish. A short piece of copper pipe can be sharpened at one end to be used to punch out foam plastic popper bodies. Plastic tampon applicators (I'm not making this up) have been used to make bluefish lures in the Long Island, New York, area. They wash up on the beaches near sewer outfalls. A clean water group picked them up and made the lures as a fund-raiser.

202 Salty anglers have substituted single hooks for the trebles on diamond-shaped deep jigs for years. They cover the tail hooks with colored surgical tubing, which defies bluefish teeth. You can make a smaller freshwater version by substituting a single hook for the treble on a casting spoon and decorating it with a plastic worm or grub, rigged weedless.

203 Chesapeake Bay striper anglers have fished "dummy lines" ever since trolling was invented. This is meat-fishing, not at all sporty. A piece of clothesline is tied to a cleat on the boat at one end and a sash weight (honest!) at the other, a sort of simple downrigger. Then a 50-pound-test leader with a bucktail jig at the business end is tied to the sash weight. Old-time anglers tied in a screen door spring for a

bit of stretch; recently, a "rubber snubber" does the same job. Huge stripers to 60-plus pounds have been caught on these meat hooks.

204 A recent sportier spin-off on the dummy line idea can be trolled on a heavy outfit. Special hefty jig molds have been made to accommodate a 12/0 hook and heavy-duty line eye. The resulting jighead weighs 2 pounds and is spear-shaped with a collar at the rear to tie on bucktail hair. The late Paul Vodak of Annapolis, Maryland, told me it took the hair from an entire buck's tail to make one of these big-fish getters.

205 The ever-popular parachute lures, shown below, composed of crinkled chartreuse nylon strands tied on a bucktail jighead in the fashion of the offshore "seawitch," often get a bit messy after use. George Bentz of Pasadena, Maryland, says: "Hold the head straight up and let the nylon hang down. Use a

Parachute lures.

hairdryer to blow air on it, and the 'hair' will lie back as it would when towed through the water. Use a comb if necessary." He then wraps his much neater lure in aluminum foil to keep it that way in the tackle box.

206 Bucktail and fly tiers can temporarily place a short section of plastic tubing over the barb and point of their hooks to keep the hook point from slicing their fingers every time the thread is wound around the hook.

207 Chrome-plated water pipe left over from plumbing your bathroom toilet makes a great lure for toothy critters like bluefish. Simply hammer each end of the pipe flat so you can drill holes for split rings to accommodate the line on one end and a hook on the other. Copper tubing, covered with highly reflective tape, has been used in the same way. Bend the pipe slightly for an enticing wiggle on the retrieve.

208 Maryland outdoor writer Bill Burton bent a piece of flat iron several times to resemble a series of "steps." In the side view, it looked like a 3-foot-long piece of flat steel shaped like two letter Ws put together. He painted it white, drilled holes in one end for an 8/0 hook, and drilled another hole in the other end for the line attachment; he trolled it for striped bass. He made two legal catches with his "lure."

209 Emergency lures or flies can be made from hooks decorated with pipe clean-

Lures made with pipe cleaners can save your fishing trip.

ers. Simply wind pipe cleaners in various colors or silver tinsel around a suitable hook, as shown opposite.

210 For extra zip, attach a spinner blade to the rear end of a lure, any fly, or an offshore trolling bait with a snap swivel by bending down the hook barb, slipping the snap swivel over it, and prying the barb back into position.

211 Any number of materials can be attached to a hook and trolled with success. Chesapeake Bay anglers once added a strip of red flannel to a bucktail jig. Later, Uncle Josh dyed pork rind strips, which have been popular for decades, were added. Offshore anglers can make a strip bait from nylon strap webbing or kerosene heater wicks.

212 Surgical-tubing lures can be made in various lengths for coastal gamefish. The tubing can be tinted in many colors with fabric dyes. Stiff stainless steel wire with a stainless steel hook at one end is threaded through the beveled end of the hose, and the opposite end is pulled back enough to attach the wire to a swivel at the "head" of the lure. The internal wire can be bent to make the lure "swim" when trolled.

213 Fly tier D. L. Goddard of Easton, Maryland, makes a reversible slider-popper by dressing a long shank hook with bucktail or feathers, then making a popper body with a tapered rear end from dense foam plastic. The eye of the hook is inserted through the lure from the rear toward the cupped face to make a popper and through the popper face toward the rear to make a slider.

214 Lure storage gets to be a problem when the angler accumulates too many baits that absolutely will be used some day. I had small and large tackle boxes of every description scattered around the garage that held an assortment of goodies that had absolutely nothing to do with one another. The way I solved the problem was described in Tackle Storage Lockers, project 23.

215 Offshore anglers have caught billfish with a rag mop–looking trolling lure with no hooks—it is simply a few strands of strong carpet yarn. Billfish wrap their bills around the "mop," and it entangles them. This is not considered "sportfishing" by many IGFA anglers.

216 I had the thought that the "hook and loop" principle might be transferred to a bass lure. Take off the hooks and cover a hard crankbait with the opposite of whatever lines the bass's mouth. If his dentures are hooky, cover the lure with loop material, or vice versa. Seems to me if a bass took a bite, the hook and loop principle might hold the fish long enough to get him in the boat—and released without even a hook wound.

Rigs

Making Rigs   217

The saltwater rigs shown opposite are as popular now as they were in 1941, when they appeared in the catalog of a long-out-of-business tackle company. They are basic, and they still work for bait fishing in freshwater or salt water. (Notice the plea on the bottom of the page, from 1941, to make striped bass a gamefish.)

However, anglers are always trying to modify or improve upon the basics. The rigs on the following pages are a few that I have found helpful. You can make them effortlessly from materials in your tackle box or from items easily obtained at your local tackle shop.

One bottom rig we find useful can be tied from a length of clear 30-pound-test Berkley Vanish fluorocarbon monofilament line. We first called it the Delaware Nothinball Rig, because that's where it originated, but since it has gained wide acceptance, we now call it the "do nothin' rig," or DNR for short. The difference in this rig is that the hook is on the end of the rig, and the sinker is threaded on the next-to-the-end loop. We find it as good for bottom fishing with bait as any commercially tied, two-hook bottom rig, easy to make, and certainly a lot cheaper.

To make the DNR, cut a 48-inch length of 20- or 30-pound-test monofilament line and tie a hook on one end (see drawing below). I use 1/0 laser-sharpened Kahle hooks for sea trout, striped bass, and croakers. Larger or smaller hooks for your specific quarry might make it necessary to increase or decrease line strength. Next, slip a 1/4-by-3/4-inch rig float on the opposite end of the line and slide it next to the hook. Then, make a dropper loop about 12 inches from the hook. (For instructions on tying knots, see the next chapter.) This is for the sinker, so make the loop large enough to accommodate the sinker you plan to use. Then, tie another dropper loop about 12 inches from the last one. Make this loop stand out about 2 inches. Slip a spinner blade and a bead or two on this loop, then thread the loop through the eye of another 1/0 Kahle hook and drop the hook point through the loop to make it captive. The top end of the rig gets a perfection loop to connect to the snap swivel on the end of the fishing line.

A swivel could also be used as a connector between line and rig. Moisten all knots

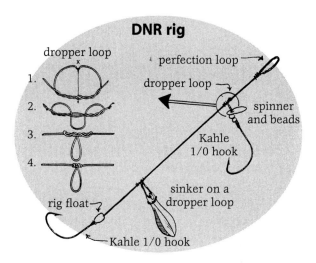

DNR rig

dropper loop

perfection loop

dropper loop

1.

2.

3.

4.

spinner and beads

Kahle 1/0 hook

sinker on a dropper loop

rig float

Kahle 1/0 hook

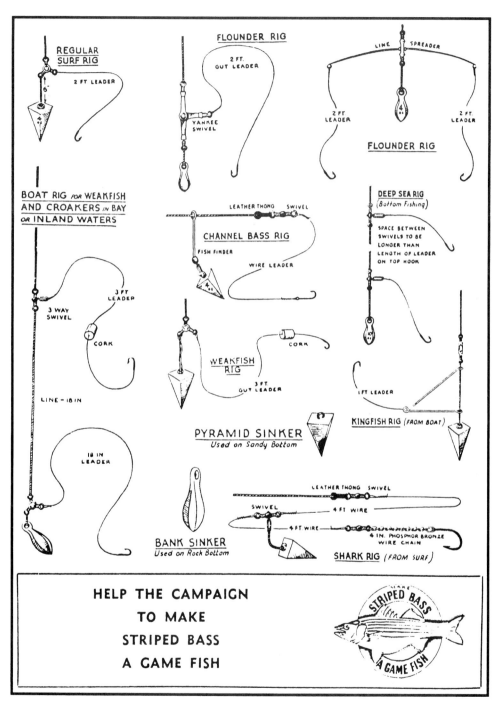

Basic saltwater rigs. This page is from the 1941 Edward vom Hofe Tackle Catalog.

before tightening them. This rig gives you short leaders and, I feel, a quicker and more sensitive connection to a fish bite. The total length of the finished rig will be about 30 inches, but this is not critical. Fish don't care about precision.

Flounder Rigs 218

"Flounderologists" are always experimenting—some in the interest of science, others trying to find the perfect rig that flatfish just can't resist. Our flounder rig has been modified again and again in recent years. What began as a simple hook baited with a minnow has evolved into a 3-foot piece of 20- or 30-pound-test leader decorated with spin-

ning blades, tied to a three-way swivel that allows for a short drop sinker. All sorts of attractors have found their way into our terminal tackle, and true believers assume these shiny, noisy additions will attract flounder.

Jack Stovall gets credit for adding a huge aluminum bass buzzbait blade in front of the hook. At Chincoteague, Virginia, Stovall bailed one flounder after another while Mark Galasso and I patiently watched. Luckily, Stovall had some extra rigs, which Galasso and I later copied for our own use.

Conventional flounder rigs are on the left side in the photograph at right. Rigs #1 and #2, designed to be dragged along the bottom, were tied by Capt. Dick Arnold of

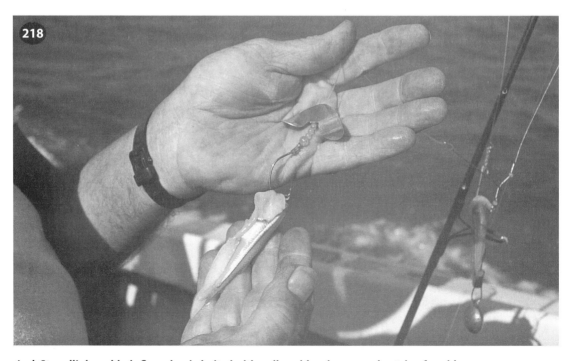

Jack Stovall's buzz blade flounder rig baited with a silverside minnow and a strip of squid.

Crisfield, Maryland. Rig #3 was a tackle shop special. Rig #4 shows Jack Stovall's buzzbait blade rig. Rig #5 was Jim Walker's change—a smaller delta-shaped blade that has less water resistance. My small in-line spinner blade decorates Rig #6. Spinner and buzz blades rotate better with two or three beads from the craft store (8 mm or so) in back of the blade. My wife insists on a brown and orange bead, buzz blade combination.

All these rigs are successful at times, although I think the flashy blades catch better. Rigs from #4 through #6 have a three-way swivel at the line end. The leader to our hooks goes on one swivel, the fishing line is attached to the second, and short

mono dropper for a sinker is tied to the third swivel. Lately, I find that a short, solid connector is better for the sinker, as it seems to tangle less.

Ultrasharp hooks tag more flounder. We use 1/0 Eagle Claw Kahle laser-sharpened hooks at leader's end. These hooks are nearly impossible to resharpen after denting them on a rock, but they will retain needle sharpness all day long in normal use. Unfortunately, they are sharp because they are made of hardened steel, which is more prone to rusting.

Spreader rigs like those shown in the top photo on page 126 are popular in some areas. The top spreader, made by Mai-Tai, has a $1/2$-ounce ball sinker at the center of

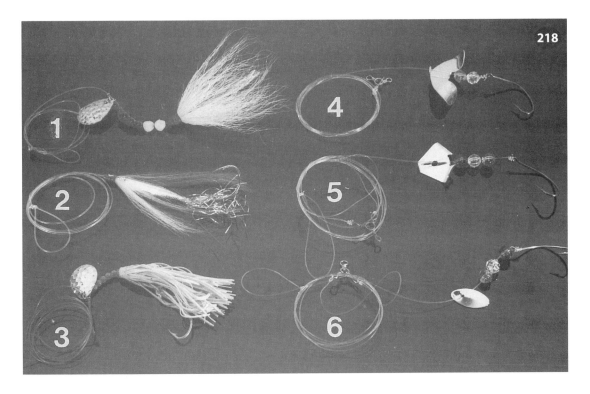

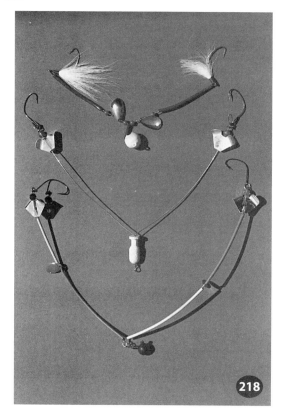

Spreader rigs.

the spreader bar. The bottom two spreaders are my combinations of weights, delta buzz blades with bead "bearings." The bottom rig also has plastic tubing covering the 0.047-inch wire spreader.

Although I haven't experimented with any of these rigs for fish other than summer flounder, their fish-catching potential for bottom-feeding minnow-chasers could be limitless.

How about trying them on other minnow-chasing bottom-feeders like walleye, sauger, perch, weakfish, sea bass—even catfish?

Bottom Rig Standoffs   219

Double- or single-hook bottom rigs are widely used to catch bottom-feeding fish. One problem that anglers often overlook is that, in using hooks with long leaders, the fish can steal a lot of bait before the slack in the long leader is stretched out and the angler can feel the fish tugging.

Conventional hook attachments on bottom rigs look like the three standoffs on the left in the photograph below. These standoffs are made from 0.027-inch stainless steel leader wire, made on a small wire bending tool sold by Netcraft.

Capt. Dick Arnold of Crisfield, Maryland, avoids the slack inherent in long leaders by attaching his hooks directly to the main line of the bottom rig. The hooks are held at a 90-degree angle to the line by drilling a hole in a plastic bead of a size that will accommodate the eye of a hook. Use a drill press, and drill the hole for the hook at 90 degrees from the existing thread hole. The bead is held in a drill press vise.

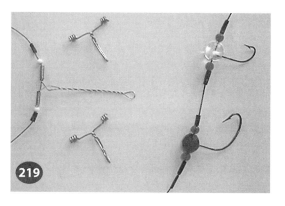

Bottom rig standoffs.

Then insert the hook into the bead, and thread the bottom rig's main line through the existing bead's thread-hole and also through the hook's eye. The bead-and-hook combo is held in place by a smaller bead on each side of the hook's bead that is in turn held captive by leader crimps. The beads on the right in the photograph are 12 mm in diameter, but hook-eye size will dictate the bead size.

When the fish tugs on these hooks, the pull is felt directly by the angler, since there is no slack in a leader.

Egg Sinker Tips 220

Egg sinkers have found a respected place in most angler's fishing gear. They are primarily used as chin-weights in rigging baitfish like ballyhoo for offshore trolling so the dead baits will swim correctly.

But over the years inshore and offshore anglers have put these versatile weights to many uses, perhaps too many for our limited space here. However, a few uses that I have found for them are listed here.

1. The top rig shown at right is mostly snag-proof. It can be used for bait fishing over rocky bottom; if the sinker gets itself into trouble, a tug slips it off the bottom wire. The snap swivel denotes the line from the reel, and the upper loop accommodates a snelled hook for the bait. An egg sinker slips onto the bottom wire, held in place by a small kink in the wire, a rubber band stuffed in its hole, or a loosely fitting wooden toothpick.

2. A way to lose the sinker and fight the fish on light tackle when a big fish bites is at bottom right in the photograph. Double your leader and slip it through the egg sinker. Double a rubber band and insert it into the leader's loop, then pull the rubber band into the sinker. A tug from the fish will pull the rubber band through the sinker, and it will drop off the line. A similar drop-off sinker rig can be made with a conventional bank sinker and a rubber band.

3. If you have a surplus of egg sinkers and need to convert them for use in bottom fishing, remove the insulation from a length of #12 copper wire. Then make a loop on one end of a short piece of the wire and insert it through the egg sinker. Bend over the protruding end and hammer it into the soft lead substitute.

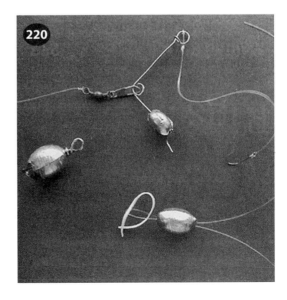

Tying Bucktail Hair on a Rivet   221

A bunch of bucktail hair on a leader ahead of a minnow or other bait can be the additional attractor that makes the fish bite. One of the best ways to make such a sliding attractor is to tie the bucktail hair on a brass rivet—not a fun job. Disposable brass rivets hold the parts of plumbing pipe compression fittings together until they are installed. The rivet spins around while you are trying to hold and tie on a hunk of loose bucktail hair. This makes for a lot of frustration but is not insurmountable.

I found that a proper diameter punch that fits tightly inside the rivet, held in a vise, will make a suitable tying jig. Jam the rivet tightly against the punch's increasing diameter.

Wrap thread around the rivet as you would when making a bucktail jig, then apply a small hank of bucktail hair at a time, wrapping it with thread until you have enough hair on the rivet to cover it. Whip-finish the thread and seal it with epoxy or superglue. On the East Coast, some call this rig a Flounder Pounder, where it is drifted along the bottom with various baits for flounder and sea trout. Favorite bucktail hair colors are white and chartreuse.

221

Pollock Rig for Shallow-Water Fish　222

Shallow-water feeders like pollock, stripers, and blues often fall for popping plugs like the one on the right in the photograph below.

At certain times of the year, however, those fish are feeding on smaller baitfish, about the size of the small bucktail jig leadered to the hookless plug on the left in the photograph, called a "pollock rig." In use, the combo is cast out and the popper is worked as usual, with short jerks of the rod tip. When fish are attracted by the noisy presentation, they often hit the small bucktail. When brought to boatside, the hookless plug serves as a handle to hold the fish steady for netting or release.

Ray Hendrickson drills a tiny, shallow hole in the plug angled toward the rear to accommodate just the tip of the jig hook. The jig is hung in the tiny hole for casting and improves distance. When cast, the combination has less wind resistance, and a shake or two of the rod tip will dislodge the jig for a normal retrieve.

Note: Substitute a foam plastic popping cork for the hard-bodied popping plug, and use a smaller jig on a similar leader to attract perch. Or, use a popping cork and a leader just long enough to keep a piece of soft crab or live baitfish above a grass bed on high water.

Pollock rig and popping plug with two treble hooks.

Soft Bait Rigs 223

Live baits like soft crabs can be held on the hook with rubber bands or the elastic sewing thread found in fabric and craft stores.

Large red drum are best tempted with a whole soft crab tied to a 7/0 hook with elastic sewing thread wound around the crab several times and tied off.

Old fishing books tell us that soft and papershell lobsters were also tied to hooks as striped bass baits along the Northeast Coast.

Rig Tips

224 As discussed in the Knots chapter, I get several feet of doubled line, sort of a "poor man's bimini knot" by tying my snap swivel on the end of a doubled line with a palomar knot (see page 138), then using a spider hitch (see page 139) 2 to 3 feet up the line to keep the doubled line together. Yep, I said "snap swivel," which upsets bass anglers. I like to change lures frequently, try new goodies. That's part of the fun of fishing, right?

225 An old tire chain, dragged slowly across the bottom at the end of a rope, can telegraph hard, rocky, or even oyster bottom, says Norm Haddaway. Finding oyster bottom is important for oyster tongers and also points out fish habitat to anglers.

226 Store your leadered flies, flounder rigs, or lures in labeled, zippered plastic bags (see photo below). Some anglers use pipe cleaners or twist ties around a coiled leader to keep it from tangling.

227 When making up leaders, many toothy-fish anglers use a trace of wire at the lure to prevent cutoffs. Others have found a bite leader can be made from a short section of braided "superline." The braided superline seems to have more resistance

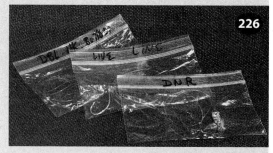

Keep flies, rigs, and lures in small plastic bags.

to sharp teeth than the fused type that sometimes frays at the business end.

228 Form a loop with the running line, pass the loop through a sinker eye, then wrap a small rubber band tightly around the loop and sinker to temporarily secure it. When a fish hits, the sinker pulls out of the rubber band wrap for a tangle-free fight. You can also tie the sinker on with a weak thread so it will break in a fish fight.

229 Tarpon anglers tie a cork float to the running line with weak thread—tarpon toss the cork in a minute. Don't use foam plastic packaging material as a float. It is not biodegradable, and it is illegal to knowingly dispose of plastics at sea.

230 Dipping the handles of wire-cutting pliers in liquid rubber makes them nonslip, even when your hands are slimy with fish gurry. Also, think about dipping sinkers in the same rubber coating to prevent dings in your boat's gelcoat—the color might even attract fish!

231 Lures rigged on leaders can be stored in plastic 16 mm film cans—found at yard sales—like those shown above.

232 In-line sinkers are often used several feet in front of crankbaits to make the lures run deeper. Tie one sinker eye to the running line and the other eye to a 3- to 5-foot leader with a shallow-running crankbait at the other end so the lure will run above the grass.

Cans for 16 mm film are the right size for rigged lures on leaders.

233 In-line sinkers used for drifting baits across the bottom usually have a 2- or 3-foot leader behind them. Make the leader of a lighter line test than the main line so it will break first in case of a snag. The same goes for trolling with a drop-sinker rig—the mono dropper should be one fourth the test of your running line.

234 Capt. Jeff Shores (see left photos on page 132) trolls seven umbrella rigs during the spring striped bass season in Chesapeake Bay. Each umbrella rig has eight hookless sassy shads trailing behind a heavy wire X. Attached to the center of each umbrella rig is a longer leader with a heavy bucktail jig (see illustration on page 132). Jeff has a way to keep these cumbersome rigs from tangling. He stores them in a waxed seafood box, separated by layers of heavy sheet plastic. One layer of plastic, one umbrella rig, and so on, until ten rigs are stored.

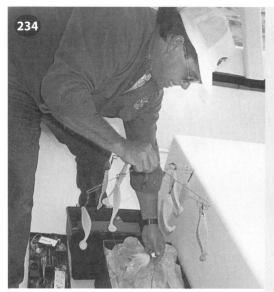

Store rigs on high-density foam plastic.

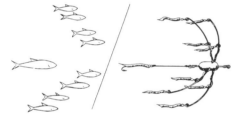

Jeff Shore's umbrella rigs. Umbrella rigs are made of stainless steel wire with four outriggers that hold teaser lures to give the appearance of a school of bait. Only the center lure is armed.

235 High-density foam plastic also makes a good place to store long leaders with hooks, flies, or jigs (see photo, top right). A piece of 1-inch-thick extruded polystyrene with several knife slits in each end for leaders makes a handy flounder rig storer. It keeps the leaders straight, too.

236 Long leaders can be kept on a piece of PVC pipe, held in place with rubber bands as shown at right.

237 Dr. Ed Hahn of Centreville, Maryland, loosely wraps a nylon cable tie around a bundle of leadered hooks and tightens the tie as hooks are removed.

PVC pipe helps keep long leaders neat.

238 Feathered hooks with an egg sinker on the leader just ahead of the "lure" can be used in an emergency as a trolling temptation offshore or inshore.

239 Tooth-defying, inexpensive lures for bluefish, king mackerel, and wahoo can be made from untwisted strands of polypropylene rope, wire-leader rigged with a 7/0 hook at the business end. Add an egg sinker at the head or a strip bait at the tail end if desired.

240 Sliding-sinker or "fish-finder" rigs can be made on the beach by hooking a bank or pyramid sinker in a snap swivel and threading the running line through its eye, then tying on a large swivel and a leadered hook. Substitute an egg sinker and have the same rig. A couple of beads between the sinker and the swivel will protect your knot.

241 Enhance slow-trolled live or dead baits by adding a flasher spoon or a spinner blade and clevis ahead of the main attraction.

242 Tie several #6 gold hooks on a 4- to 5-foot leader of 30-pound-test mono with a sinker at the end and bait the hooks with a tiny piece of fish, and you'll catch all the bottom-feeding baitfish you need for near-shore king mackerel and other gamefish.

243 If you don't have cut bait for your multi-hooked baitfish rig, tie a bit of bucktail or feathers on the hooks to imitate smaller baitfish.

244 Small, ¼-inch-diameter colored hoses armed with 1/0 hooks spaced 8 to 10 inches apart on a 30-pound-test leader ended with a 4- to 6-ounce diamond jig will attract Atlantic mackerel by the cooler load. The macks are not only good to eat, but frozen chunks of mackerel are a great bluefish bait in the surf. Check out the spring schedule for Atlantic Ocean head boats. Take a big cooler.

245 Frank Daignault ties a heavy metal jig into the leader ahead of a featherweight swimming plug for added casting dis-

tance—this setup keeps the plug swimming a bit deeper, too.

246 Tie a treble hook on the leader several feet ahead of a trolled swimming plug to catch and accumulate weeds that would foul your line.

247 A quick gipsy rig can be made by tying a three-way swivel to the end of the fishing line. The other two eyes of the swivel get different lengths of leader ended with lures of your choice.

248 Craft shops are the usual places we find beads for our rigs. Think about buying cheap costume jewelry at yard sales for the same purpose.

249 Dave "Peanut" Sullivan of Berlin, Maryland, developed the Eastern Shore Quik Rig, shown here, for surf and bottom fishing. Spaces between the top and bottom wire coils allow the angler to "wind" line or leader around without removing the sinker. "No knots, slippage, or line cutting," Peanut says.

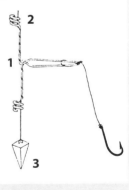

Dave Sullivan's Eastern Shore Quik Rig.

250 "Float fishing" for king mackerel, we use the rig shown on page 134, made from 6 feet of 40-pound-test braided wire with a swivel and balloon float at one end and a three-way swivel at the other end. Two 1/0 stainless steel treble hooks on wire droppers complete the rig—both inserted in the live baitfish. Kings rarely miss both hooks.

Balsa floats could be substituted for the balloons by using large rubber bands around the float to capture several passes of running line that release when the fish hits.

251 Try a floating jighead behind or above a sinker when drift-fishing. It floats above the bottom, and since fish usually strike upward, it could gain you a few bites.

252 A popular rig passed on by the (Chesapeake) Bay Country Bassmasters is a Carolina rig with an egg sinker ahead of two beads, then a swivel, and a 2-foot leader followed by an air-impregnated plastic salamander on a 5/0 worm hook.

Our float-fishing rig for king mackerel.

253 Ted Sheridan rigs a worm weight backward ahead of a swivel stop, then ties on a 2-foot leader terminated by a worm hook and a green Mr. Wiffle. "Deadly on spotted sea trout," Ted says.

254 If you run out of brass sinker eyes when pouring up some large in-line or bell-trolling sinkers, skin some #14 copper wire and wrap short sections of it around a finishing nail (head up) in a vise. Leave short "pigtails" to grip the lead inside the sinker.

255 Bob Meushaw tied the rigs shown opposite for the feather jigs he made during the striped bass heyday on Chesapeake Bay. When the stripers were feeding on silverside minnows, Bob lobbed this rig out (it can tangle when it is cast hard) and let it sink into a school of breaking fish. By whipping the rod tip, the feathered jigs "danced" around like escaping baitfish. Very effective!

256 Downrigger weight tail fins can be bent to one side so they will run farther outboard when trolled, thereby keeping them apart on turns.

257 Fly anglers often mark their lines with a Sharpie pen where enough line has been stripped in for another cast. For night fishing, Tom Fote of Toms River, New Jersey, overwraps the same place with fine thread and smoothes it over with Pliobond. When stripping in a fly at

Bob Meushaw's rig for striped bass

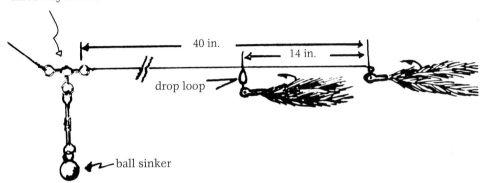

three-way swivel

40 in.

14 in.

drop loop

ball sinker

night, Tom can feel the proper "stop" as it passes through his fingers.

258 A similar overwrap with a stopper bead below it serves as a check for a sliding float to provide the proper depth for a bait. Make up a few of these knots on pieces of tubing and leave the ends long. After slipping the tubing to the proper spot on the fishing line, slip the knot off the tubing and pull the ends to tighten the knot.

259 Jim Walker's rig for live-baiting stripers consists of a rotating hook standoff above a 6-ounce sinker. The swiveling standoff with beads above and below it will keep the rig from tangling. Its short-leadered hook holds a live spot or white perch. Very effective!

260 Keep each different size of hook or snap swivel on a large snap swivel. It reduces tackle box clutter.

261 Loop-to-loop connections or swivels between leader and line won't go through the rod guides. Wind-on leaders allow the angler better fish control at boatside. Special splices are needed for wind-ons. Check with your local tackle shop for the proper tools.

262 Wrap wire solder around a lure's hooks to make the plug run deeper or to make a "floater" into a "submerger."

263 Wear heavy leather welder's gloves when handling wire leaders with big fish attached.

Knots

The following pages include drawings of several basic knots (courtesy of Stren and Ande) I have found helpful in my fishing. Here are a few guidelines, starting with line selection.

264 Don't buy cheap line. Midpriced lines give the best performance for the dollar. Line is one of the cheapest items in fishing; don't skimp on quality.

265 Practice tying knots. Start with a piece of clothesline if that will help you to visualize how a certain knot will look when tied in a small-diameter line.

266 Select lines for the use you intend to give them. For the type of fishing I do, it boils down to two types: monofilament and fused gel-spun polyesters—sometimes called "superlines."

267 My personal preference is to use mono lines for almost all angling. I use the improved clinch knot and the uni-knot for mono lines. Always moisten a mono line knot before tightening it.

268 Manufacturers of "superlines" recommend the palomar knot for minimal slippage. Better yet, get the advantage of additional abrasion resistance by doubling 2 or 3 feet of line and tying a palomar knot at the snap swivel or lure and a spider hitch 2 or 3 feet up the line.

269 Always check the line for nicks or abrasions that will cause a weak spot. If you find abraded or nicked areas, check your rod guides to make sure they are not the culprit.

270 Cut off 20 or 30 feet of line after fighting a big fish, and retie your knots.

271 When it's time to change your fishing line, dispose of your old line in a safe, responsible manner. Never throw worn-out line overboard where it can create a fatal trap for fish and wildlife. Set an example for your companions.

272 To learn more about knot tying and fishing line, check the bibliography in the Resources chapter for recommended reading and sources.

Blood Knot

The best knot for tying two lines together of about the same diameter.

Improved Clinch Knot

1. Pass line through eye of hook, swivel, or lure. Double back and make five turns around the standing line. Hold coils in place, thread end of line through first loop above the eye, then through big loop, as shown.

2. Hold tag end and standing line while pulling up the coils. Make sure the coils are in a spiral, not lapping over one another. Slide tight against eye. Clip tag end.

Dropper Loop

This forms a loop in the middle of another wise knotted line, giving you a place to attach a hook, sinker, or fly. Though this is not a strong knot, it is useful with panfish and small saltwater species.

1. Form a loop in the line.

2. After eight to ten turns, reach through the center opening and pull the remaining loop through. Keep your finger in this loop so the loop will not spring back. Hold loop with teeth and pull both ends of line, making turns gather on either side of loop.

3. Set knot by pulling lines as tight as possible. Tightening the coils will make loop stand out perpendicular to the line.

1. Double about 4 in. of line and pass loop through eye.

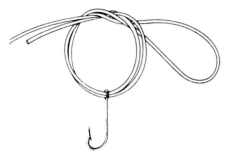

2. Let hook hang loose and tie an overhand knot in doubled line. Avoid twisting the lines, and *don't tighten.*

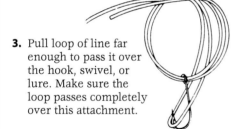

3. Pull loop of line far enough to pass it over the hook, swivel, or lure. Make sure the loop passes completely over this attachment.

4. Pull both tag end and standing line to tighten. Clip tag end.

Perfection Loop

A perfection loop knot is used at the ends of the leader belly and the tippet.

1. Double the end of the leader belly forming a loop about 6 in. long. Form a smaller loop about 2 in. from the end of the leader belly so that the smaller loop is behind the doubled line.

2. With the larger loop, make a wrap around the smaller loop and pass the end of the larger loop through the smaller one.

3. Wet the knot area and firmly pull the larger loop. Be sure the wraps tighten evenly. Trim excess.

4. To connect the perfection loops, pass the tippet loop over the lure through the leader belly loop. Clip tag end.

Spider Hitch

This is a fast, easy knot to create a double-line leader. Under steady pressure it is equally strong but does not have the resilience of the bimini twist under sharp impact. Not practical with lines above 30-pound test.

1. Form a loop of the leader length desired. Near the point where it meets the standing line, twist a section into a small reverse loop.

2. Hold small loop between thumb and forefinger with thumb extended well above finger and loop standing out beyond end of thumb.

3. Wind double line around both thumb and loop, taking five turns. Pass remainder of large loop through the smaller one and pull to make five turns unwind off thumb.

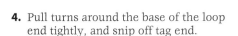

4. Pull turns around the base of the loop end tightly, and snip off tag end.

Surgeon's End Loop

Use this knot to tie a loop in the end of the line for attaching leaders or other terminal tackle quickly.

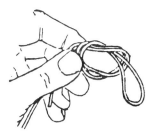

1. Double the end of line to form a loop, then tie an overhand knot at the base of the doubled line.

2. Leaving the loop open, bring the doubled line through once more.

3. Hold the standing line and tag end, and pull loop to tighten knot. You can adjust the loop size by shifting the loose knot before tightening. Clip tag end.

Surgeon's Knot

This knot joins a leader to a line. Unlike the simplified blood knot, it effectively joins lines of varying diameters.

1. Lay line and leader parallel, overlapping 6 to 8 in.

2. Treating the two like a single line, tie an overhand knot, pulling the entire leader through the loop.

3. Leaving the loop of the overhand open, pull the tag ends of both the line and leader through again.

4. Hold both lines and both ends to pull knot tight. Clip ends close to avoid foul-ups in rod guides.

The Uni-Knot System

This system uses one basic knot for a variety of applications. The uni-knot can be varied to meet virtually every knot-tying need in either freshwater or salt water. Developed by Vic Dunaway, editor of *Florida Sportsman* magazine and author of numerous fishing books including *Vic Dunaway's Complete Book of Baits, Rigs, and Tackle.*

Tying to Terminal Tackle

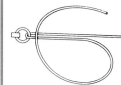

1. Run line through eye of hook, swivel, or lure at least 6 in.; fold to make two parallel lines. Bring end of line back in a circle toward hook or lure.

2. Make six turns with tag end around the double line and through the circle. Pull standing line to slide knot up against eye. Tighten knot. Clip tag end.

Snelling a Hook

1. Thread line through hook eye about 6 in. Hold line against hook shank and form uni-knot circle.

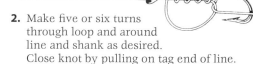

2. Make five or six turns through loop and around line and shank as desired. Close knot by pulling on tag end of line.

3. Tighten by pulling standing line in one direction and hook in the other. Clip tag end.

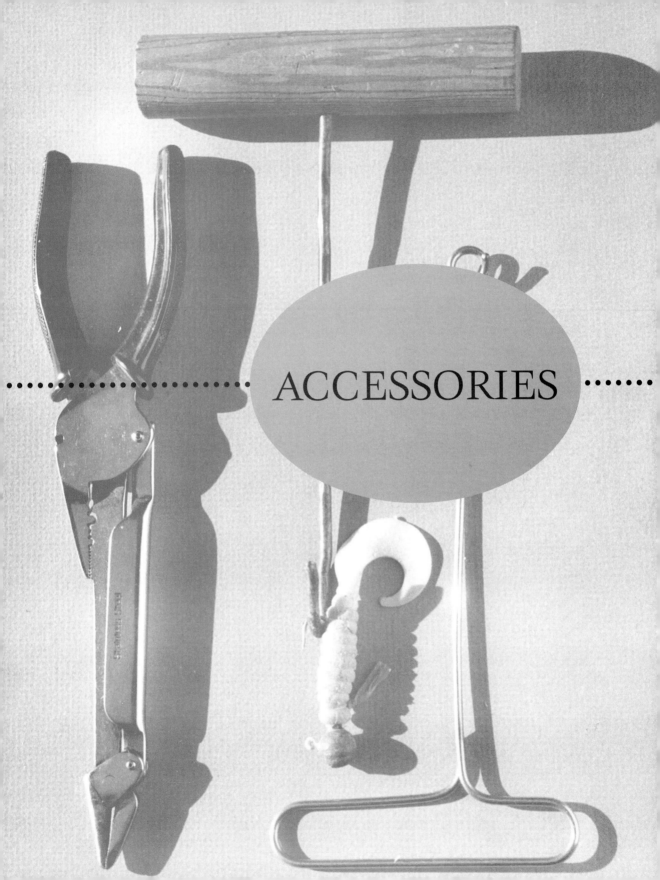

ACCESSORIES

Pier Carts 273

Pier fishing regulars use all sorts of wheeled vehicles to transport their tackle, coolers, lunch, bait, and sometimes even umbrellas out onto the longer piers.

On Maryland's Choptank River at Cambridge, two fishing piers were made when the center of an old bridge on Route 50 was removed. Fall fishing for sea trout is best at the far ends, near the channel—either 4,400 feet or 2,200 feet from your car—and walking to the far end of either pier with a load of gear is easier with a cart.

"I think it was a fantastic idea to make a fishing pier out of this old bridge," says Herbert Gough, below, who frequently fishes and crabs from the Fishing Piers at Cambridge.

Gough has built himself a unique wheeled combination fishing tackle carrier and umbrella-shaded chair to transport his gear on his many Maryland fishing pier trips.

Grocery carts and little red wagons are often pressed into service to haul fishing gear onto piers like the Seagull Fishing Pier at the Chesapeake Bay Bridge-Tunnel across the mouth of Chesapeake Bay.

273

Fred Sharkey and Tom Goldston of Norfolk, Virginia, in photograph above, fish the Seagull Fishing Pier. They spread their seven rods along the railing on the T-end of the Seagull Pier. "We catch good numbers of 3-pound croaker here," Sharkey said, "and there are spot and gray trout aplenty in summer." Spring and fall see runs of mon-

273

fishing necessities that has rod holders on each side.

Baitfish can be kept alive in laundry or peach baskets with a lid lowered in the water—or in white buckets with battery-powered fish aquarium aerators.

American ingenuity also comes into play in getting one's hooked fish from the water up onto the pier. Small fish are no problem to lift up to pier level. On lower piers, a long-handled gaff will hoist the biggest blue-fish. But, on higher piers, regulars have de-signed hoop nets that can be lowered on parachute cord for medium-sized fish, and "bridge gaffs" made from giant weighted tre-ble hooks on stout cord are used to snag and raise bigger fish.

Rig a Golf Cart for Bassin'   274

Bass anglers who fish in lakes know their fa-vorite fishing holes are just that—big holes in the ground, filled with water. So, it stands to reason that if someone digs holes in the ground, sooner or later they will fill with water and someone will stock bass in them.

Which leads us to golf courses—perhaps the largest untapped source of bass fishing anywhere. When bulldozers pile up all that earth to make greens, sand traps, and the like, they leave a hole, or "borrow pit." When the pit fills with water, it becomes a "water hazard," an abomination to golfers, but when stocked with bass, it's the Promised Land to anglers.

Along every golf course, picturesque lakes and ponds provide pleasant scenery,

ster bluefish pass the Seagull, and these an-glers use a live spot floated under a balloon for the choppers. Sometimes a 40- or 50-pound cobia will hit the suspended spot.

Another suggestion for hauling fishing gear out onto piers is a wheeled cooler for ice, tackle, food, and fish. One chap made a cart to tow behind his bike, allowing him to easily transport all the gear he needs.

I use a regular two-wheel delivery dolly to carry tons of tackle and a huge ice-filled cooler down the dock to the boat. Beach an-glers sometimes use a child's plastic snow sled—they attach a box to accommodate water hazards to entertain golfers, and great habitat for bass and other stocked fish.

On a Florida golf course, I met Joe Anderson from Pennsylvania, who had a golf cart rigged just the way a nongolfing angler would want it. In place of golf bags on his cart, Anderson mounted fishing rod holders in back of the seat. A huge Phantom tackle box rode on the rear platform. Weather curtains and a radio were added for comfort. And, best of all, it had a trailer hitch. On a golf cart! Anderson had a small boat and trailer he moved around his favorite golf course from one (fishing) hole to another.

Golf etiquette dictates: "Wait until they play before moving up, and try not to make distracting motions or loud noises when a player gets ready to hit the ball."

We followed groups of golfers around the course in our bassin' cart until we saw a neat place to fish, then we stopped. We hid our carts behind bushes and behind the golfer's line of sight.

I see a fertile field to plow out there: golf course managers opening up at 5 A.M. so anglers can fish the water hazards before the first golfer tees off; bait and tackle in the golf pro shop; pro bass tours from course to course; and bass guides in golf carts. The new sport of golf cart bassin' is virtually untapped. Rig a golf cart for bassin' and go for it.

Make Your Own Side Planers　　　275

Side planers, like outriggers and downriggers, can place the angler's lures into hard-to-get-at-places or into shallower water than the boat or propeller will tolerate—and still allow the use of light tackle. They also get your lures away from the boat's wake.

My inexpensive side planer was made from 1-inch-by-8-inch pine shelving and a few items from the hardware store. Two boards are required for each side planer. Mine are about 24 inches long, so an 8-foot board would make two complete planers, one each for port and starboard.

The first item of business is to cut off the front end of each 24-inch board at about a 20-degree angle, like the bow of a ship. The longest dimension will be the top of the planer when it is in the water.

Then, that cut must be beveled at about

The author temporarily rigged this golf cart for bassin'.

a 45-degree angle so the board will travel away from the boat. The beveled edge will always face toward the boat. Sit the board upright on its shortest edge and imagine how water pressure would act on the bevel, and you will see which side of the boat it will travel away from.

The unit described here is designed to run off the starboard side. If you make side planers for the port side, reverse the 45-degree bevel so the beveled edge faces toward the boat.

After your 20-degree angle and the 45-degree bevel cuts are made, offset the two boards about 7 inches and C-clamp them together, as shown below, on the workbench.

The next task is to mark, drill, and place two 1½-inch-long ¼-20 (¼-inch diameter by 20 threads per inch) stainless steel studs in

the *bottom edge* of each board—for a total of four.

1. From the unbeveled end of the *protruding board* (rear board in the photograph below), measure 2 inches and strike a pencil line across both boards while clamped together.

2. Strike another line across both boards about 2 inches from the beveled edge of the *nonprotruding board* (front board in photograph below).

3. Mark a 1-inch depth on a ¼-inch drill bit with a piece of masking tape, and drill holes 1 inch deep at the center of each board edge on your pencil lines.

4. Mix a small amount of epoxy and place a dab in each hole to secure a stud. Place a

275

¼-20 Nylok nut on the tip of each stud to keep epoxy off the threads, and place each stud about 1 inch deep into these holes.

5. Let the epoxy set up overnight.

Next day, with the boards still clamped together, turn them over and strike lines across them from edge to edge so the stud holes you have just made will line up with the stud holes you are about to drill in the opposite edge.

Repeat the marking, drilling, and setting of studs on the *top edge* of each board. Now you have four studs epoxied into the top edge of the boards and four studs epoxied in the bottom edge.

While the epoxy sets up, cut four 12-inch-long pieces of ⅛-by-¾-inch aluminum or stainless steel bar stock. Drill a ⁵⁄₁₆-inch hole ½ inch from the end of each piece of stock.

When the epoxy has set up, place two predrilled aluminum bars on the studs from the top edge of one board to the top edge of the other board and two bars on the bottom edges of the boards as shown in the photograph at right. With the boards set on edge and their slanted ends in a position like the bow of a ship, place stainless steel ¼-20 wing nuts on the top studs and ¼-20 Nylok nuts on the bottom studs. Snug the nuts down to allow only a slight amount of movement of the bars. The wing nuts are used to lock the unit in place folded flat for storage or opened up for use.

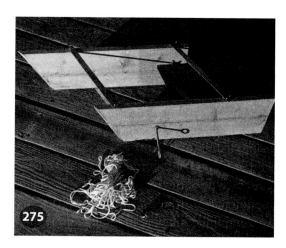

275

Next, drill a ¼-inch hole about 4 inches down from the top edge and about 8 inches back from the "prow" of the outside surface of the board nearest to the boat (with the beveled edge nearest). Place a ¼-20 stainless nut and washer on a 6-inch eyebolt about halfway up, and put the eyebolt through the hole. Put a washer on the inside of the bolt, and run a ¼-20 Nylok nut down the threads until it is flush with the end of the threads. Then tighten the nut nearest the eye until the eyebolt is tight and snug.

Disassemble all your parts and place them in order of disassembly. Paint the boards with two coats of epoxy (I used West System), allowing for drying between coats.

At this point, decide whether to apply a coat of blaze orange paint for visibility or whether to mount a small blaze orange flag on top of each unit so people trolling near you can see the side planer. The final finish is up to you, but don't use the blaze orange spray that utility technicians use to mark buried power or phone lines under your lawn. That product washes off as you troll the unit in water. It is biodegradable and water soluble. I know.

In use, 50 to 100 feet of parachute cord is tied to the eyebolt and connected to a midpoint on your boat. (Some anglers have a bow-mounted pole with two huge reels on it, one for each unit, port and starboard. Others simply tie the line to the after end of the bow rail as a temporary rig that can be easily removed.).

When the sideriggers are deployed, the simple line-release device shown below can be used to carry your fishing line to the side planer and place your lure out of the engine's slipstream or over shallow areas where your prop would be in serious jeopardy.

Make up several line-release clips as shown in the photograph; each will include a shower curtain ring and a small alligator clip from a local electronics store, plus a ½-inch-diameter circle of ⅛-inch sheet rubber or plastic. Cement or epoxy ½-inch disks of sheet rubber or plastic to each side of an al-

ligator clip's jaws to hold your fishing line. Drill a hole in the clip's base to accommodate the shower curtain ring.

When trolling, as in the photograph above, if you have two sideriggers, they are placed to port and starboard. When they are deployed, line-release clips are clipped to the rod's line, allowing 30 or so feet of line between clip and lure to make a "leader." Then, open the shower curtain ring and slip the line-release clip over the line to the side planer. Let the clip slide down the parachute cord to the side planer. When a fish hits the lure, the line is pulled out of the clip and the fish can be fought on light tackle.

It is not necessary to bring in the side planer each time you catch a fish. Simply reclip the fishing line to another siderigger clip and send it down the parachute cord to the side planer again. A supply of release clips can be stored aboard for the possibility that you might find a mother lode of willing fish.

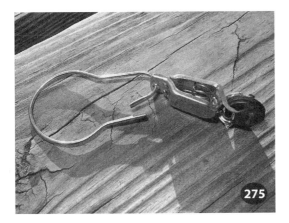

Planers as Downriggers   276

Planers are often used to take lures down to suitable depths. One problem with planers is they exert a lot of pressure on the tackle, and an angler must use 30-pound gear or heavier to control even a medium-sized lure-planer combination. When a fish strikes the lure on a leader behind the planer, the planer "trips" and relieves the downward pressure so the fish can be reeled in much easier.

Planers are effective, no question, but there is another way to use them so the angler can fight the fish on light tackle.

276

First, rig the planer on a heavy line; even clothesline will do, but parachute cord would be strong enough and its thinner diameter will cause less friction. Mark the line every 10 feet and keep track as you let the planer out so you can repeat the depth if you get a strike.

You can buy line-release clips or make

them from inexpensive parts, as we did in project 275.

Next, rig a line release in the aft hole of the planer. In use, the fishing line (light tackle is fine) is clipped in the release, and the reel's line sent down on the planer. When a fish strikes, as with a downrigger, the line snaps out of the release, and the fish can be fought on light tackle. A jerk on the planer line will trip it so it can be retrieved and reset.

Dockside Fish Cleaning Table   277

A 5-gallon plastic bucket attached to a kitchen sink cutout makes a good temporary fish cleaning table for your dock. Simply turn the bucket upside down and place it over a dock piling, and you're ready to fillet fish (see photos, opposite). Remove it for storage if necessary. When we built our pier, the dock pilings were left at a convenient 32-inch height above the decking, just right for fish cleaning.

Kitchen sink cutouts have a nice plastic laminate on a plywood base. I attached the bucket to the bottom of the cutout with four screws through the bottom of the bucket and spray painted the bucket black to match the creosoted piling. Lath strips around the edge of the laminate top keep fillets from slipping overboard.

Kitchen installers usually have the cutouts. Drywall contractors, bakeries, and farmers are good sources for surplus plastic buckets.

The author installing his fish cleaning table.

Cleaning fish.

A Cup Holder for the Tow Car 278

Car cup holders are available from most auto supply stores, but I never found a size or configuration that suited my needs or my vehicle. So, I made two holders of $^5/_{16}$-inch plywood, one for my station wagon tow car and another for my wife's sedan.

Overall outside dimensions are $9^7/_8$ inches long by $4^5/_8$ inches wide by $7^1/_2$ inches high. Each cup compartment is $4^3/_8$ inches square to contain the insulated plastic mugs so popular today—and there is a $1^1/_4$-inch-

wide handle slot that extends from the top to within $^1/_2$ inch of the bottom of each cup compartment (see photo on page 150).

For rear-wheel-drive cars with a "drive train hump," you can make a thin card-board pattern to fit the round hump at the spot where the holder will be placed. This pattern will indicate the correct radius for the holder's bottom. Front-engine vehicles have either a small hump or none at all. Adjust your bottom configuration accordingly to fit the floor.

I traced the tunnel hump pattern for my station wagon on the plywood, then mea-

pocket with some regularity. They're never around when you need them.

On my boat, fishing towels are held in place with plastic shower curtain rings. Plastic rings hold up better in the marine environment, and they don't leave rust marks on your boat's gelcoat as do rings made of steel. Plastic rings become brittle when exposed to sunlight for several months, but they are inexpensive and easily replaced.

sured and marked the wood for cutting the side pieces. Ends, separator, and the bottom were measured and cut.

The pieces of wood were squared up and joined with small finishing nails and glued joints. The unit was stained and varnished. I added a small detachable, compartmented plastic box (made for school lockers with a 3-by-3-inch sheet magnet attached) to the front side of the mug holder. Next, I glued a piece of sheet metal to the front side of the wood holder to attach the plastic box by its magnet. This attachment holds a vehicle log for business mileage, small notepad, pens, pencils, and a small calculator.

Fast or brake-jamming drivers can line the bottom curvature of the cup holder with hook-and-loop material to keep the unit in place in heavy stop-and-go traffic.

A Simple Fishing Towel Hanger 279

Fishing towels seem to migrate around a boat, beach buggy, or out of a beach angler's

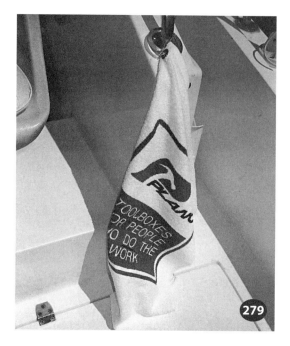

Simply punch a hole near one corner of a suitable fishing towel or use a sewing machine to make a buttonhole on the towel, insert the shower curtain ring, then slip that ring around a bow rail, grab handle, cooler handle, surf belt, or any other convenient location.

Many advertising towels already have a brass grommet.

Rod Handle Fishbonker 280

An embarrassing incident left a 15-inch-long piece of 1-inch-diameter hardwood trolling rod handle in my gunwale rod holder. Hefting the cleanly broken-off handle, it seemed that the handgrip was comfortable. If I added some weight to the broken end and a thong near the grip for safety, I would have an inexpensive fishbonker.

I drilled a ⁹/₁₆-inch hole about 6 inches up into the center of the broken end of the handle and made some rough angled holes inside the larger hole with a small drill bit to hold the poured lead substitute in place.

Later, when I had the pot heated to pour some sinkers, I clamped the handle in a vise and filled the hole in the handle with molten lead or lead substitute. The trick here is to have the material just hot enough so that it will pour, but not as hot as you would like it for making jigs or sinkers. If the material is too hot, it will ignite the wood of the handle.

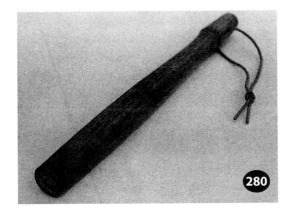

Rod handle fishbonker.

⚠ **When working with lead, always work in a well-ventilated area, and wear very heavy gloves so you won't burn your hands. Lead fumes can be toxic. Be careful pouring, too—a pocketful of hot lead is nothing to sneeze at. See also the safety tip on page 105.**

Last, I drilled a ¹/₄-inch-diameter hole through the grip end for a thong. Cotton cord could be wrapped around the handle for a nonslip grip.

My rod handle fishbonker is economical, easy to make, and is just the right size for pacifying medium-sized saltwater gamefish like king mackerel and lunker bluefish.

Fish Flipper 281

Fish that are unpleasant or dangerous to handle with bare hands can be easily unhooked and flipped into the fish box or overboard with a simple buttonhooklike device. To make a "fish flipper," start with a 12-inch-long piece of ¹/₈- or ⁵/₃₂-inch-diameter stainless steel rod and bend it so that a ¹/₂-inch-deep and ¹/₂-inch-wide hook is formed at one end of the rod. The stainless steel rod is bent by placing two 16-penny common nails vertically about ³/₈ inch apart in a vise (with their heads, not their points, exposed for safety) to make a bending jig. Insert the rod between the nails about ³/₄ of an inch and use the longer part of the rod for leverage to make the bend.

A handle at the other end of the rod can be as fancy or simple as needed. For those who have machining facilities, a fancy handle can be made from a 4-inch-long piece of ⅝-inch-diameter stainless steel bar stock that is then welded to the rod to form a T-shaped handle or drilled and tapped so the rod can be threaded and screwed into the handle.

A wooden handle can be made from a 4-inch long piece of 1¼-inch-diameter closet rod or dowel, as shown in the photograph below. Drill a hole through the dowel that is a neat fit for the rod, push the rod through the hole, then make a U-shaped bend in the rod and drive the rod down into a shallow hole drilled into the top of the wood handle. If the rod is a little loose, a dab of epoxy will tighten it up.

In use, fish are flipped off the hook by grasping the flipper's handle in one hand and the hook's leader in the other (see illustrations opposite). With the device's hook engaging the leader, the two are pulled away from each other until tight. When the flipper's hook engages the fishhook, the fish is given a rotary motion around the leader. The fish comes off the hook easily. The method works well for single fishhooks but is not recommended for trebles.

When fish to be released are deeply hooked, there are several ways to get the hook out so the fish won't die. Most are based on the premise the hook can be

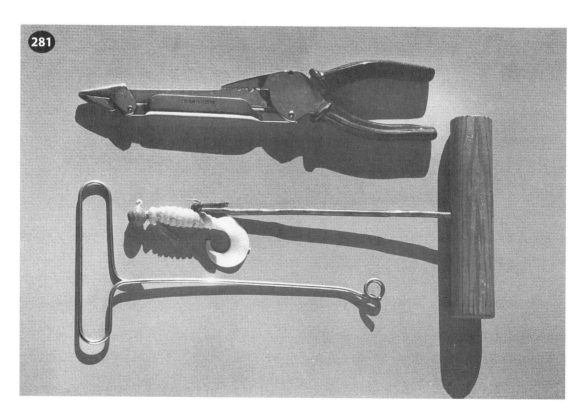

Dehooker

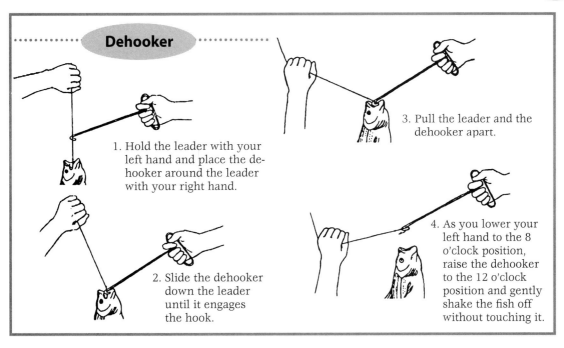

1. Hold the leader with your left hand and place the de-hooker around the leader with your right hand.

2. Slide the dehooker down the leader until it engages the hook.

3. Pull the leader and the dehooker apart.

4. As you lower your left hand to the 8 o'clock position, raise the dehooker to the 12 o'clock position and gently shake the fish off without touching it.

Deep Throat Dehooker

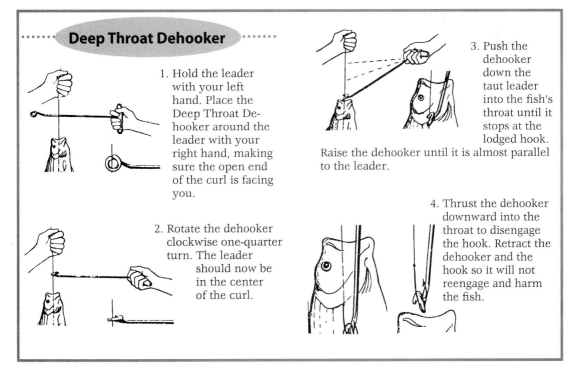

1. Hold the leader with your left hand. Place the Deep Throat De-hooker around the leader with your right hand, making sure the open end of the curl is facing you.

2. Rotate the dehooker clockwise one-quarter turn. The leader should now be in the center of the curl.

3. Push the dehooker down the taut leader into the fish's throat until it stops at the lodged hook. Raise the dehooker until it is almost parallel to the leader.

4. Thrust the dehooker downward into the throat to disengage the hook. Retract the dehooker and the hook so it will not reengage and harm the fish.

backed out of a fish's gut and then retrieved through its mouth. Barbless hooks make this more feasible, but this advice also includes barbed hooks.

Another deep hook retriever is a long-nosed plier like the top item in the photo on page 152. Others include a flat piece of strap metal with a V-shaped notch in one end that engages the hook and forces it to back out of fish flesh, then engages the hook for easy removal.

My favorite is a Deep Throat Dehooker (the bottom item in the photo on page 152) consisting of a ¼-inch-diameter piece of wire with a formed handle at one end and a "pigtail" at the other. The pigtail, or curl, is open enough to engage a hook leader and let it slide down to the hook, whereupon the angler jabs it slightly downward to back the hook out of fish flesh as shown in the illustration on page 153. The hook then "hides" in the pigtail so the angler can remove the hook from the fish's gullet. These are sold in fishing tackle shops.

Studies in Chesapeake Bay indicate deeply hooked fish should have those hooks removed if at all possible to lower mortality.

Marker Buoys 282

Buoys can be purchased to let us mark the spot where we find fish, wrecks, structure, or bottom contours. The H-shaped buoy on the right in the photograph is a factory-made marker buoy. It is suitable for small waters, since its small size dictates it can only be seen for a short distance.

On big bodies of water such as the

Chesapeake Bay, a larger buoy is needed for good visibility. Even in rough water, a big jug can be hard to spot from a distance.

The buoy on the left in the photograph below was made from a 1-gallon yellow antifreeze jug, about 60 feet of heavy twine, and an old duck decoy weight. The yellow jug is visible for long distances. Sixty feet of twine suits me, since I rarely fish in water more than 45 feet deep. Just about any heavy weight that will keep the jug in place would work.

Don't rely on someone else's jug to find you fish, though. Some rascals purposely toss their marker jug several hundred feet away from the action. (Refer to A Double Buoy for Precise Anchoring, project 105.)

GPS and loran plotters may soon phase out the old reliable jug markers, but the jugs still work in a pinch.

Combination Lure Retriever and Boat Hook 283

A 6-foot aluminum crab net handle was still in good shape when its wire netting rusted away. It was too good to toss out.

I made a combination lure retriever and boat hook from the net's aluminum handle, a brass snap, a screw eye, two wood plugs, two plastic furniture leg tips, and some epoxy.

283

First, I cut off two 2-inch pieces of wood dowel that fit neatly inside the aluminum handle. A pilot hole was drilled in one end of one wood dowel to accept the screw hook. A plastic tip was slipped over the handle, and the screw hook was threaded into the wood.

⚠ **Round off the point of the hook with a file or grinder! Store it where the hook won't hurt anyone.**

The other dowel was epoxied into the opposite end of the aluminum handle, which was drilled out to accommodate the swivel end of the snap. Before the epoxy to anchor the snap set up, I slipped one plastic tip over the handle, then inserted the snap into the dowel.

283

To retrieve hung-up lures, clip the snap over the fishing line and slide it down the line to the lure. The length of the handle limits the depth at which a lure can be retrieved. When the snap reaches the hung lure, jiggle it around until the lure is free.

The opposite end of the combination tool can be used to grab docklines and handle other boat hook duties.

Chumming Gear   284

Chumming, the act of using all manner of fish food to attract fish to a baited hook, is used all over the world in freshwater and salt water. Most common chum ingredients are mashed shellfish or ground fish but also include veggies like corn and rice, macaroni, dog and cat food, and even pieces of whatever is being used for bait at the moment. There are many ways to deliver chum to the fish, some of which are illustrated in the chumming gear shown below.

An old meat grinder like the one at top center in the photograph below can be found at a garage sale or flea market. In Florida and other locales where chumming is popular, large food grinders are mounted on boards and belt-driven by electric motors. Garbage disposal units have been used, but the danger here is that water and electricity are too close together, and an electrician should rig such a unit. Large-scale (no pun intended) chum vendors use a garden chipper (honest!), which is incredibly dangerous.

Chumming gear.

Ground chum can be frozen, but just like bait, fresh is best. In the Chesapeake Bay and other areas, anglers often grind up fish carcasses after filleting the fish—then freeze the chum in 2-inch-deep aluminum cake pans with slanted sides that will release the frozen block. This yields a flat chunk of chum, which fits in laundry, onion, or citrus fruit bags (far left in the photograph) tied to the boat's transom on the fishing grounds. As the frozen chum melts, it filters through the bag and forms a "chum slick" that attracts fish. Large mesh bags are best.

Another piece of equipment to hold chum is a 5-gallon plastic bucket with ½-inch holes drilled around the bottom third of the bucket to disburse the chum. Hang it off the transom—it will disburse the chum evenly. If you have a bucket minus the holes, use a ladle to distribute the chum, but you must maintain a solid chum line without breaks or you will lose the fish.

A minnow trap (top left in the photograph), a cricket cage (center, with rope attached), or a homemade galvanized rat wire cage with a door can be used to hold and disburse chum.

To make the PVC pipe chum pot (at the bottom of the photograph), cut a 3-foot length of 4-inch-diameter sewer drain-field pipe, drill several lines of ½-inch holes in it, and attach an end cap to one end with PVC cement. Then, drill a hole in the center of that end cap and one other end cap to accommodate a piece of bungee cord that acts to keep the unit closed after filling it. Make a loop on each end of the bungee cord: one for a sinker (or a sinker could be placed in-side the unit) and one for a line attached to your boat. These chum pots can also be attached to your anchor rode where it meets the anchor chain before anchoring or hung from the transom. Dry, nonodorous chum can be purchased if the angler has an uneasy stomach.

Cat food makes great chum for bottom-feeders like flounder, weakfish, croaker, and perhaps others in the freshwater realm that one might anchor to fish for. Buy the kind with a pull ring to open the can; attach a snap swivel to the ring, and add enough line to reach the bottom. Jim Walker of Bozman, Maryland, says he outcaught some of the locals using this idea. He caught sea trout while they caught nothing. They all laughed—he ate trout that night.

To wrap up this discussion, consider the chaps who use modified hair curlers as chum holders (I'm not making this up. It was reported by esteemed outdoor writer Bill Burton in the *Capital* in Annapolis, Maryland). Hair-curler chum pots are designed to upend and distribute their load of chum after they are shot with a slingshot to bait an area. A light line is affixed so the curler can be retrieved. Look up this neat carp info on the Internet. Chumming technology has hit the carp-fishing world. What next?

Tiny Chum Pot 285

A tiny chum pot made from a plastic film canister can put a small amount of chum right next to a bottom-fishing angler's hooks. The author's rig, shown on page 158, is intended to attach to the bottom of a two-hook bottom rig where the sinker would normally attach. The sinker then would go on the bottom of the chum pot rig. A small amount of ground fish or cat food goes into the canister, and the lid snapped on. Dissolving chum leaks out through holes in the canister.

To make the rig as pictured, drill holes in the center of the top and bottom of the film canister and its cap. Then, punch ¼-inch-diameter holes around the sides of the canister. A piece of monofilament leader material (this rig uses 100-pound-test mono) is inserted through the canister and its lid and attached to a large snap swivel under the bottom of the canister to hold a sinker. A loop is formed above the top of the canister and closed with a crimp sleeve.

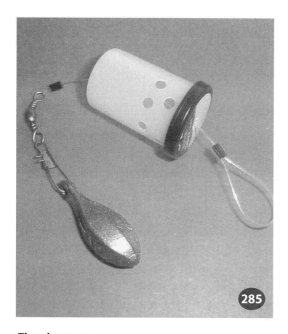

285

Tiny chum pot.

Accessory Tips

286 Place a strip of reflective tape on net handles, tackle boxes, and gaffs—or anything else you may want to find at night. Or, tape a flashlight to the net handle.

287 Take the plastic tip off the end of your net handle and stuff the inside with foam packing peanuts. Tamp them in with a dowel. See if the net floats. It usually will. You can also fill the handle with the canned foam insulation used around house windows; fit a small piece of tubing on the spray head, and fill the handle from one end, letting the foam expand to fill the handle. Break off any overflow after it cures.

288 Handle toothy fish with crab tongs, available in areas where tidewater crabbing exists.

289 Dr. Ed Hahn hangs a fly strip on the boat when biting flies are a problem.

290 Carry one or two "emergency blankets" on the boat in cold weather. They are made from aluminized Mylar, which reflects body heat back to the person wrapped in them. They are usually available in camping or sporting goods stores.

291 Use a foam can cooler to store a ¼-pound spool of fishing line as in the photograph opposite. The foam cooler keeps the line from unspooling

291

A foam can cooler is storage for a spool of fishing line.

and out of the sun's injurious rays. I keep a spool of 30-pound-test clear Ande line on the boat for leaders and to make up bottom rigs.

292 Hang plastic grocery bags in your boat cabin for trash (they'll blow away if hung outside). Use plastic hooks with adhesive backing to hang the bags.

293 An old shoelace or a piece of 100-pound-test monofilament leader can be used to anchor your fishing hat in a breeze. Some anglers cut a length of mono line to fit around their neck and attach each end to both bows of their eyeglasses as a keeper.

294 Keep spools of leader on a piece of bungee cord attached at each end to a convenient spot in your boat. Some anglers rig a plastic box to hold several spools of leader material by drilling holes in the side of the box and labeling the monofilament exit holes.

295 On open boats in the winter, what I call a "basser's face mask" is a lifesaver. The protector has a Velcro strap that goes around the head and fits over glasses, caps, rain suits, and other gear. It is a great face shield in a fast boat. Called a *boater's vision visor* in bass fishing supply catalogs, it costs about $20.

296 Pouring outboard oil into a reservoir inside the boat's hull can be messy. Use an antifreeze pourer available in auto parts stores for this task. It will have a twist-type shutoff valve and about 12 inches or so of clear plastic tubing. Mine exactly fits the screw top of a 1-gallon plastic bottle of TC-W3 outboard oil.

297 Stainless steel size 11 crochet hooks can be used to pick out backlashes on reels. Just by having one aboard, you won't get backlashes, guaranteed.

298 Big-water anglers often carry huge nets for large gamefish they may want to release. In the Chesapeake Bay, they store these nets on top of the cabin. My tip? Anchor the net with bungee cord in rough water or when running.

299 Keep a balloon or two inflated and tied to a piece of monofilament long enough to reach bottom with a barbless hook on the other end. When a school fish like black drum is caught, hook the fish with the balloon rig and release it. Capt. Buddy Harrison of Tilghman Island, Maryland, follows a school of drum all day that way. Rubber balloons will biodegrade, Styrofoam coffee cups will not. Consider the environment—enough said.

300 Build your own minnow, eel, or crawfish trap from galvanized hardware cloth. Roll a 24-by-20-inch piece into an 8-inch-diameter cylinder to make the unit, then make a funnel for each end. Use aluminum wire in freshwater to sew the cloth together, or use heavy mono line in salt water.

301 A tall plastic trash can is useful on a boat as a fly line stripping basket. Anchor the basket with bungee cord or a little water in the bottom, and leave 10 feet or so of fly line in it as a guide for the next retrieve.

302 Grass shrimp are great baits for just about any saltwater gamefish. They can be kept alive longer by building several "picture frames" of 1-by-1-inch stock and stapling plastic window screen to them. Grass shrimp are spread out on the screen, and the frames are stacked in a cooler until needed. Don't let water cover the shrimp.

303 Keep sea worms and live eels from direct contact with freshwater or ice in the cooler with a plywood or foam plastic baffle.

Resources

Bibliography

Dunaway, Vic. *Vic Dunaway's Complete Book of Baits, Rigs, and Tackle.* 13th ed. Miami: Wickstrom, 1998.

Pfeiffer, C. Boyd. *Modern Tackle Craft.* New York: Lyons & Burford, 1993.

Tackle Component Suppliers

Bass Pro Shops
2500 E. Kearney
Springfield MO 65898
800-BASSPRO (800-227-7776)
www.basspro.com
   Lure components, molds, hooks, and accessories. Mainly freshwater-related tackle.

Cabela's
1 Cabela Dr.
Sidney NE 69160
800-237-4444
www.cabelas.com
   Rod and lure-making supplies, fly tying, and other sporting goods.

Jann's Netcraft
3350 Briarfield Blvd.
Maumee OH 43537
Orders only: 800-NETCRAFT (800-638-2723)
Information: 419-868-8288
www.jannsnetcraft.com
   Rod, lure, and fly-tying supplies, and books. Molds, accessories, tools, and other items.

Offshore Angler
2500 E. Kearney
Springfield MO 65898
800-4-OFFSHORE (800-463-3746)
www.offshoreangler.com
   Saltwater rigging materials and tools. Baitwells and other supplies, plus offshore accessories.

Orvis
1711 Blue Hills Dr.
Roanoke VA 24012
800-548-9548
www.orvis.com
   Fly-tying materials and tools, accessories, and fishing tackle.

Boat and Fishing Supplies

BoatU.S.
3665 E. Bay Dr., Unit 124
Largo FL 33771
800-937-2628
www.boatus.com
   Boat accessories and fishing tackle. Retail stores nationwide, plus catalog sales. Memberships available.

Boater's World
1010 W. Fort Macon Rd.

Atlantic Beach NC 28512
800-826-2628
www.boatersworld.com
   Boat accessories and fishing tackle. Retail stores nationwide, plus catalog sales.

West Marine
P.O. Box 50070
Watsonville CA 95077
800-BOATING (800-262-8464)
www.westmarine.com
   Boat accessories and tackle. Retail stores nationwide, plus catalog sales.

Metric Conversions and Trademarks

Metric Conversions

feet x 0.3 = meters
inches x 25.4 = millimeters
yards x 0.9 = meters

Trademarks

3M, Ande, Atom, Bait Runner, Berkley, Blazer, Boone, Boston Whaler, Cabela's, Chevrolet, Chug Bug, Cordell, Creek Chub, Culprit, Dacron, Danforth, Darter, Deep Throat Dehooker, Do-It, Dodge, Dremel, Drydene, Evinrude, Exxon, Fathom-Master, Ficht, Fin-Nor, GlobalMap, Gudebrod Bros. Champion Silk, Guide Series, Heddon, Herter's, Igloo, Jet-Dry, Johnson, Kahle, KotaStow, Lowrance, Lures by Atom Pure Fishcology, Luxor, Mako, MapTech, Mercury, Minn Kota, Montgomery Ward, Mr. Wiffle, Mylar, Netcraft, Never Seez, Nylok, OMC, Penn, Phillips, Plano, Plexiglas, Pliobond, Polaroid, Powerwinch, Rat-L-Trap, Rebel, Rust-Oleum, Sharpie, Shimano, Stanley, Starcraft, Storm Lures, StowAways, STP, Stren, Styrofoam, Sunbrella, Suzuki, Teflon, Tiny-Trap, Uncle Josh, Velcro, WD-40, and West System are registered trademarks.

Index